Cambridge Elements ☰

Elements in the Philosophy of Religion
edited by
Yujin Nagasawa
University of Birmingham

PANTHEISM

Andrei A. Buckareff
Marist College, New York

CAMBRIDGE
UNIVERSITY PRESS

University Printing House, Cambridge CB2 8BS, United Kingdom

One Liberty Plaza, 20th Floor, New York, NY 10006, USA

477 Williamstown Road, Port Melbourne, VIC 3207, Australia

314–321, 3rd Floor, Plot 3, Splendor Forum, Jasola District Centre,
New Delhi – 110025, India

103 Penang Road, #05–06/07, Visioncrest Commercial, Singapore 238467

Cambridge University Press is part of the University of Cambridge.

It furthers the University's mission by disseminating knowledge in the pursuit of
education, learning, and research at the highest international levels of excellence.

www.cambridge.org
Information on this title: www.cambridge.org/9781108457507
DOI: 10.1017/9781108558266

First published 2022

A catalogue record for this publication is available from the British Library.

ISBN 978-1-108-45750-7 Paperback
ISSN 2399-5165 (online)
ISSN 2515-9763 (print)

Cambridge University Press has no responsibility for the persistence or accuracy of
URLs for external or third-party internet websites referred to in this publication
and does not guarantee that any content on such websites is, or will remain,
accurate or appropriate.

Pantheism

Elements in the Philosophy of Religion

DOI: 10.1017/9781108558266
First published online: February 2022

Andrei A. Buckareff
Marist College, New York

Author for correspondence: Andrei A. Buckareff, andrei.buckareff@marist.edu

Abstract: This Element focuses on some core conceptual and ontological issues related to pantheistic conceptions of God by engaging with recent work in analytic philosophy of religion on this topic. The conceptual and ontological commitments of pantheism are contrasted with those of other conceptions of God. The concept of God assumed by pantheism is clarified and the question about what type of unity the universe must exhibit in order to be identical with God receives the most attention. It is argued that the sort of unity the universe must display is the sort of unity characteristic of conscious cognitive systems. Some alternative ontological frameworks for grounding such cognitive unity are considered. Further, the question of whether God can be understood as personal on pantheism is explored.

Keywords: pantheism, god, metaphysics, mind, religion

ISBNs: 9781108457507 (PB), 9781108558266 (OC)
ISSNs: 2399-5165 (online), 2515-9763 (print)

Contents

1 Introduction

God in western theism is often understood as ontologically *other*. Most analytic philosophers of religion characterize God as being both transcendent and the one to whom all things in our universe owe their existence. Yet, perhaps paradoxically, God is also understood as immanent and omnipresent, being near us, even *in* us, in some sense. There is no shortage of imagery and metaphors offered to represent the nearness of God. They range from medieval mystics using erotic language to describe encounters with the divine to contemporary evangelical Christians referring to God as their friend who "lives in their heart." But most theologically sophisticated adherents to the Abrahamic religions usually fall short of emphasizing divine immanence and omnipresence so much that they identify God or some aspect of God with the universe. This is most likely due to the influence, however indirect, of what is often referred to as "traditional theism."

In contemporary philosophy of religion "traditional theism" picks out that metaphysics of the divine on which God is understood as being the omnipotent, omniscient, omnipresent, morally perfect, eternal, creator, and sustainer of the universe. *Qua* creator, God is additionally taken to be wholly ontologically independent of God's creation. Finally, many proponents of traditional theism take God to be a nonembodied *person*.[1] Of course, there is no shortage of debates over how to think about these various divine attributes and their compatibility with one another. Alternatives to traditional theism, such as pantheism, deny that God possesses one or more of the aforementioned attributes.

Given that my focus here is on pantheism, I will not be concerned with any other alternatives to traditional theism (such as pan*en*theism), except to point out where they contrast with pantheism. Regarding pantheism and traditional theism, the central commitment of traditional theism that the pantheist denies is the assumption that God is ontologically independent of the cosmos. God is taken by the pantheist to be identical with the totality of existents. What the precise implications of this sort of identity claim happen to be is a matter of some dispute and will be discussed in later sections of this Element.[2]

---

[1] Perhaps the most prominent recent presentation and defense of the doctrine of divine personhood is Richard Swinburne's (1993). For critiques of Swinburne's case for divine personhood that vary with respect to whether or not God should be understood as personal, see Davies 2016, Thatcher 1985, and Hewitt 2019. For a general defense of exploring alternatives to traditional theism, see Bishop 1998.

[2] Some have denied that pantheism is committed to such an identity claim and have maintained that if God and the universe stand in a constitution relation to one another (with either God constituting the universe (Effingham 2021) or the universe constituting God (Coleman 2019)), then that is sufficient for pantheism. I offer reasons for rejecting this claim in Section 2.

The term "pantheism" comes from the combination of the Greek *pan* (all, every) and *theos* (god). Pantheism as a conception of God has an ancient pedigree,[3] but it has always been a minority view. The term "pantheism" is itself of relatively recent origin. John Toland (MacIntyre 1967/2006; Mander 2020) is often credited with first coining the term in 1705. While Toland was the first person of whom we are aware to use the English term, "pantheism," Joseph Raphson first introduced the concept (using the Latin term "pantheismus") in 1697 – eight years before Toland – in his work *De Spatio Reali seu Infinito*. Toland had commented upon Raphson's work. So Toland was certainly familiar with Raphson's use of the concept (Suttle 2008, 1342).

Given the relatively recent origin of the term "pantheism," it may be anachronistic to identify a figure in the history of philosophy and religion as having embraced pantheism. Moreover, some figures are sufficiently ambiguous to at least make a pantheistic interpretation of their position plausible. Furthermore, outside of the west and India in the common era, it is not at all clear that the views of some figures are best identified as pan*theistic*. Given the controversies that accompany historical commentary, in this work I shall mostly avoid any discussion of historical figures. Any discussion of historical figures in this Element will only be to help shed light on current thinking about contemporary pantheistic proposals in debates over the metaphysics of the divine. And my focus will be fairly narrow. I will attempt to situate pantheism as a metaphysics of the divine within the context of contemporary analytic philosophy of religion. More narrowly, still, I will be largely preoccupied with whether a suitable account of the unity of the cosmos can be delivered that will provide us with the truthmakers for treating the universe as the divine mind. Therefore, in what follows, I will be engaging almost exclusively with the work of analytic philosophers and framing my treatment of pantheism against the backdrop of recent debates in analytic philosophy of religion, philosophy of mind, and metaphysics.[4]

My primary goals in what follows are conceptual and metaphysical and not epistemological. I am most interested in distinguishing pantheism from other ways of conceiving of God. And I am concerned with exploring what the world must be like in order for pantheism to be a tenable metaphysics of the divine. Any epistemological implications of what I am doing here will have to do with the *prima facie* reasonability of pantheism as a coherent metaphysics of the

---

[3] In the west, the earliest proponents of a pantheistic conception of God might have been the Stoics (Baltzly 2003).

[4] I recommend that readers interested in the work of various historical figures on pantheism begin by consulting William Mander's (2020) excellent entry on "Pantheism" in the *Stanford encyclopedia of Philosophy* and go on to examine Michael Levine's (1994) seminal lengthy survey of pantheism (1994) as well as T. L. S. Sprigge's (2006) magisterial study of the metaphysics of the divine that pays considerable attention to pantheistic proposals.

divine that is consistent with a scientific worldview. Therefore, while there is interesting work to be done on what reasons we have for believing that the pantheist God exists, I cannot do these matters any justice in this Element.

I will proceed as follows. In Section 2, I will focus on clarifying the concept we have in mind when we are talking about pantheism. Next, in Section 3, I will discuss the question of what kind of unity the universe must exhibit to be a candidate for being identical with God. I will argue that it must exhibit the sort of cognitive unity characteristic of minds. In Section 4, I will consider some candidate ontological frameworks that might deliver cognitive unity. I will then, finally, turn my attention to the question of whether God can be personal on pantheism. Owing to constraints of space, I will not take up challenges to pantheism in the various sections in any depth. Moreover, there are a host of other topics I cannot take up here owing to limitations of space.

2 Clarifying What We Could Mean by "Pantheism"

In his tome on pantheism, Michael Levine identifies "the central problem of pantheism" as determining what is meant by "pantheism" (1994, 25). I take it that any account of what is meant by "pantheism" will assume that it is a metaphysics of the divine on which God is identified with the cosmos. Conceptions of God on which the cosmos is part of God but on which God's being does not share the ontological boundaries of the cosmos, are pan*en*theistic.[5] The distinction between these approaches to conceiving of the divine is often glossed over. Moreover, some ways of characterizing pantheism even fail to distinguish it from some versions of traditional theism. In this section, I will attempt to clarify the pantheistic conception of God in a way that renders it distinct from other conceptions of God that are panentheistic or variants of traditional theism.

2.1 First Attempt

Suppose we follow Spinoza and say that "Whatever is, is in God, and nothing can be or be conceived without God" (1677/1985, E1p15, 420).[6] If such an understanding of the relationship between God and the cosmos is taken to be sufficient for pantheism, then we get something like the following definition for "pantheism."

---

[5] For this reason, I take Nikk Effingham's (2021) proposal on which God constitutes the universe but whose being may extend beyond the cosmos to fail to count as pantheistic but rather as a sort of inverted pan*en*theism.

[6] I do not wish to assert that Spinoza is best read as a pantheist. For an argument for reading him as a pan*en*theist, see Melamed 2018.

(PAN$_1$) Pantheism=$_{df.}$ Everything is in God and nothing can be or be conceived apart from God.

PAN$_1$ fails to deliver a conception of God that is a genuine alternative to some variants of traditional theism. The basic idea expressed in the definition is found in orthodox Jewish and orthodox Christian thinking about the divine.

PAN$_1$ as a statement of God's relationship to the world is expressed in the Jewish Medieval liturgical poem, *Shir ha-Yihud* (שִׁיר הַיִּחוּד) which is sometimes translated as "Hymn of Unity," "Hymn of Oneness," or "Song of Unity." The most relevant parts of the poem express a relationship between God and the cosmos on which all that exists is somehow internal to God. Divine immanence is described using imagery that calls to mind how God is described in PAN$_1$: "Thou encompasses everything and fillest everything; and being everything, Thou art in everything." And the inseparability of what there is from God is clearly expressed: "And Thou art not separate and apart from everything, no space is void and free from Thee" (Friedlander 1888, 28). The Jewish philosopher, Moses Maimonides, hardly a pantheist under any description, in his *Guide for the perplexed*, describes the ontological dependence of the cosmos on God thusly: "[I]t is through the existence of God that all things exist, and it is He who maintains their existence by that process which is called emanation. . . . If God did not exist, suppose this were possible, the universe would not exist. . . ." (1190/1904, 104). Similar sentiments are found in the Christian tradition. The Apostle Paul, in his oratory before Stoic and Epicurean philosophers at the Aeropagus, described God as the one in whom "we live and move and have our being" (Acts 17:28 NRSV). And, much later, in his *Institutes of the Christian religion*, John Calvin asserts that "our very being is nothing but subsistence in the one God" (1559/1960, Book. I, Chapter 1, 35).

Whether or not Spinoza was influenced in his thinking about how God relates to the cosmos by such statements as the foregoing is unimportant. What is important is that the sort of account of God's relationship to the cosmos we get from PAN$_1$ is not sufficient for pantheism. The conception of God we get with PAN$_1$ is *consistent* with pantheism. Moreover, it may articulate some implications of a different, better formulation of pantheism. But *it is not sufficient* for pantheism.

There are two claims made in PAN$_1$ about God's relationship to the cosmos. First, everything is internal to God in some sense. Second, nothing can exist or be conceived apart from God. I will refer to the first claim as the "internality hypothesis" and the second as the "conceptual-dependence hypothesis." Neither of these is separately nor jointly sufficient for pantheism.

The internality hypothesis has been taken by some to be a direct implication of a proper understanding of divine omnipresence and omnipotence. We find this way of thinking about God's relationship to the cosmos expressed in multiple places in the orthodox theistic cannon in philosophical theology. For instance, Anselm of Canterbury expresses this idea quite clearly in Chapter XXIII of his *Monologion* when he writes that "The supreme nature exists in everything that exists, just as much as it exists in every place. *It is not contained, but contains all,* by permeating all" (1066/1998, 40).

More recently, Robert Oakes (2006 and 2012) has gone to great pains to distinguish *theistic internalism* from *theistic consubstantialism.*[7] According to theistic internalism, the universe is somehow internal to God. According to theistic consubstantialism, the universe and God are essentially made of the same stuff,[8] with God being either identical with or wholly constituted by the cosmos. While theistic consubstantialism implies theistic internalism, Oakes argues that the converse is not the case. He argues that theistic internalism is implied by two divine attributes, namely, divine omnipresence and divine omnipotence. Regarding omnipresence, there is no ontological room, Oakes argues, for natural objects that are "ontologically *exterior* to a Being Whose plenitude is absolutely limitless" (2006, 174). With regard to omnipotence, Oakes asserts that divine omnipotence must include the power to produce objects interior to God (2012, 71). Elsewhere, I have argued that a commitment to theistic internalism, when coupled with certain other commitments about the nature of divine omniscience, commits one to theistic consubstantialism (Buckareff 2018). I will not rehearse my argument here. Rather, I will simply register my agreement with theistic internalists like Oakes that a commitment to theistic internalism, on its own, does not imply a commitment to theistic consubstantialism. If it does not commit us to theistic consubstantialism, then it does not commit us to pantheism. Moreover, even if it did imply a commitment to theistic consubstantialism, it does not follow that theistic consubstantialism implies a commitment to pantheism. Theistic

---

[7] Views on God's relationship to the world that are motivated by a particular understanding of divine omnipresence that can be described as variants of theistic internalism can be found in Hudson 2009, Pruss, 2013, and Swinburne 1993.

[8] I have used the locution "stuff" rather than referring to God and the universe being identical with or constituted by the same "substance" in the interest of avoiding attributing any particular ontological commitments to either pantheistic or panentheistic conceptions of the divine. It is not obvious that substance monism is an ontological commitment of either account of the divine (see Levine 1994 and Johnston 2009). For that matter, I do not wish to suggest that either is committed to substance as an irreducible ontological category. Process theists, who are panentheists, reject the category of substance outright in their ontology (see Whitehead 1929). Either conception of the divine is consistent with a range of ontological commitments regarding the primary ontological categories.

consubstantialism is neutral between pantheism and panentheism (where, by "panentheism" I mean any metaphysics of the divine on which the universe is a part of God but is not identical with God). Thus, the truth of the internality hypothesis does not suffice for the truth of pantheism.

As for the conceptual dependence of all things on the concept of God, this sentiment is rarely expressed as clearly as in PAN$_1$. But it is often implied. For instance, if nothing can exist apart from God and God cannot be conceived as not existing, then whatever exists cannot be conceived as existing apart from God. This seems to be a direct implication of Chapters III–IV and XIII of Anselm of Canterbury's *Monologion* (1077/1998). Again, such an understanding of how things are conceptually dependent upon the concept of God is not unusual in traditional theism. Like the internality hypothesis, the conceptual-dependence hypothesis does not suffice to get us to pantheism.

While neither hypothesis is individually sufficient for pantheism, might they be jointly sufficient? No. All that we get from the conjunction of the two is an understanding of God that is not uniquely pantheistic but is, rather, commonly expressed by traditional theists who expressly reject pantheism. That said, both of these hypotheses may be direct implications of pantheistic commitments. I will leave this question for now and will turn to consider some alternative definitions of "pantheism."

2.2 Second Attempt

Suppose that I am right that it is uninformative to be told that pantheism is the doctrine that everything is in God and depends upon and cannot be conceived apart from God. Will the following definition be an improvement (Mander 2020)?

(PAN$_2$) Pantheism=$_{df.}$God is everything.

PAN$_2$ definitely distinguishes pantheism from traditional theism given that traditional theists will reject saying that God is everything. But it does little to distinguish pantheism from pan*en*theism. The reason why is that we can understand the "is" in "God is everything" in terms of *either* identity or constitution. More clearly, PAN$_2$ is ambiguous between the claims that God is *wholly constituted* by everything (but *not* identical with everything) and that God is *identical* with everything. Moreover, further distinctions can be made between different ways to understand what the intended referent of "everything" is and how things must fit together in order for everything to be God. But that is something we will wait to take up in subsections 2.3 and 2.4. For now, it is worth noting just how uninformative PAN$_2$ is. In particular, I wish to focus on the just-mentioned fact that it is ambiguous between an identity claim and a constitution claim (assuming that constitution is a relation that is different from identity). Let me explain.

Suppose that by "everything" we mean to refer to all of the existents in the universe. If God is wholly constituted by everything, then God and the universe are distinct coinciding entities that share all of the same properties. Some of these properties are essential properties of God's and are merely accidental properties of the cosmos, and vice versa. A consequence of this is that God and the cosmos have different persistence conditions. So in assuming that God is everything, where the "is" is the "is" of constitution, then the conception of God that is correct would be panentheistic.[9] This view can be contrasted with the pantheistic claim that assumes that God is *identical with* everything (where by "everything" we mean the entire cosmos). Nothing about the divine being transcends the universe on such a view. Yet, again, assuming that by "everything" we mean the totality of existents in the universe, both views can assert that "God is everything." So how important is it that we insist on understanding pantheism as being committed to God's being *identical* with the universe?

Consider the claim that God is identical with everything. I suggest that, in discussing pantheism and identifying God with everything, we restrict the extension of "everything" to the universe. Why do this? Failure to do this, again, will result in our failing to distinguish pantheism from panentheism. A panentheist can accept that God is identical with everything if everything includes entities that go beyond those that are constitutive of the universe. Charles Hartshorne underscored this difference between pantheism and his own preferred process version of panentheism. He noted that what makes God divine is distinct from the "cosmic collection" that is the universe (1948, 88). This is so for at least two reasons. First, "The divine personal essence ... infinitely transcends the de facto totality ..." (Hartshorne 1948, 89). That is, the divine is not limited to the totality of existents that we identify with the universe. Second, Hartshorne notes that "the essence of God is compatible with any possible universe" (Hartshorne 1948, 89). In light of the difference, he suggests that "panentheism" is the best term to pick out the metaphysics of the divine on which God is "in some real aspect distinguishable from and independent of any and all relative items, and yet, taken as an actual whole, includes all relative items" (Hartshorne 1948, 89). Hartshorne's position is perfectly compatible

---

[9] See Johnston 2009 for a presentation of this sort of panentheism on which God is constituted by the physical universe. See Buckareff 2016 and 2019 for critiques of this sort of view of God as well as arguments for why we ought to accept pantheism over such a panentheistic conception of the divine.

with the claim that God is identical with everything where everything may be constituted by more than the cosmos.

Thus, there are least two reasons we should resist taking pantheism to be the thesis that "God is everything." First, if we limit the extension of "everything" to be all that exists in the universe, it could be true that God is everything, but God is not identical with everything (being wholly constituted by the universe in the aforementioned sense). Second, "everything" could include more than the cosmos, and God could be identical with everything, but the conception of the divine that results would, again, be panentheistic rather than pantheistic.

So, if we take pantheism to be the metaphysics of the divine on which God is everything, there are two assumptions that we must make. First the "is" in "God is everything" is the "is" of identity, not constitution. Second, "everything" is the totality of existents constitutive of the universe.

2.3 A Better Definition

Given the foregoing, I suggest that we accept the following as the working definition of "pantheism" for the purposes of this Element:

> (PAN$_3$) Pantheism =$_{df.}$ God is identical with the totality of existents constitutive of the universe.

This definition is not ambiguous in the ways that the previous two definitions are. PAN$_3$ would be rejected outright by both the traditional theist and the panentheist. For the former, it would be because it fails to respect the ontological cleavage between the creator and creation. For the latter, it would be because the "is" of identity expresses the wrong sort of relationship between God and the cosmos.

On PAN$_3$, pantheism is taken to be the thesis that God is only identical with those existents that are together constitutive of the universe and nothing more. But is this too restrictive? If it is not, what more might be included among the totality of existents? I propose that we restrict our focus to variants of pantheism that are consistent with ontological naturalism and *at least* a modest realism about the objects in our experience (where by "modest realism" I mean the metaphysical theory that holds that our representations of things in the world countenanced by the various sciences can be true even if there is not a one-to-one correspondence between the existents that make our representations true and the representations themselves). I will argue that this focus is not too restrictive. Rather, it provides us with some boundaries to help guide our inquiry in what follows. Given the assumptions of ontological naturalism and modest realism, the constituents of the universe will be the sorts of existents that are consistent with our experiences and best scientific theories. Hence, we get a principled basis for the boundaries and for determining what would fall outside of them.

If we are going to understand pantheism as a metaphysics of the divine that is committed to a version of ontological naturalism, then a definition of "ontological naturalism" is needed. Here we must tread carefully, we need a definition that is neither too restrictive nor too liberal. The schema I will offer is based on a definition given by David M. Armstrong according to which ontological naturalism is the hypothesis that "reality, the whole of being, is constituted by the spacetime world" (1999, 84). So, consider the following:

> (OntNat) A theory T is ontologically naturalistic if and only if T does not countenance the existence of any entities that are not constituents of the spatiotemporal system that is the universe.

If ontological naturalism is correct, then the world is the universe. Regarding the restrictions placed by this definition on what counts as a naturalistically admissible entity, entities such as Platonic Forms and other abstracta that are assumed to be nonspatiotemporal are regarded as nonnatural (as most of their proponents would admit). Hence, assuming the circumscribed parameters of what sorts of things are admissible in our ontology given OntNat, such things are precluded from being among the existents in the world.

A further advantage of OntNat is that it is a view that does not admit of entities that have more or less being. What is, simply is. Any actual objects are *real* objects. Assuming OntNat, there are not also, contra Alexius Meinong (and those sympathetic to proposals like his), *ideal* objects (1904/1960, 78–81). The only ontological status an entity has is either existing or not. There is not a recherché third category of being such as Meinong's *bestehen* ("subsistence" – which, in contrast to existence, is a timeless mode of being).

A further advantage of OntNat is worth noting. While OntNat provides some parameters for what sorts of entities are admissible assuming ontological naturalism, it is more liberal than some other definitions of ontological naturalism. For instance, OntNat does not entail physicalism (by "physicalism" I mean the hypothesis that everything is physical in the sense of being the sort of entities whose nature is exhaustively described by a complete physical theory). OntNat leaves it an open question whether or not there are natural objects, properties, and laws involving them that are not physical in the relevant sense.

It may be argued that OntNat is too restrictive. For instance, it may preclude some recent pantheist proposals such as István Aranyosi's "logical pantheism" (2013). On Aranyosi's metaphysics of the divine, God is identical with logical space. First, logical space, on his account, is the "space of the Absolute

Everything" (Aranyosi 2013, 9). The space of Absolute Everything is larger than the space of all possible worlds (although logical space contains all possible worlds). It is the largest conceivable space. He refers to this as the thesis of "Logical Totalitarianism" (Aranyosi 2013, 13). Importantly, on logical pantheism, there is no such thing as existing *simpliciter*, but only "*existing-relative-to-a-region-of-logical space.*" And for an object, *a*, to exist-relative-to-a-region-*R*-of-logical-space is simply for *R* to depict *a* as being some way. For example, Pegasus exists-relative-to-Schwine's-surroundings, which means that the story figuring Schwine depicts Pegasus as an existing winged horse (Aranyosi 2013, 25).

There is more to Aranyosi's logical pantheism that I will ignore given that the remaining details are not relevant for my purposes here. For now, notice that if God is identical with logical space then such a metaphysics of the divine is not an ontologically naturalistic account of the divine given OntNat. What exists is not exhausted by what is in spacetime. Moreover, things do not exist *simpliciter*. Their being is relative to a region of logical space. The metaphysics of the divine that we get on logical pantheism fits comfortably in the same metaphysical neighborhood as Meinongianism about objects. But this is an allegedly pantheistic proposal. Given OntNat, I am suggesting we take logical pantheism to lie outside of the boundaries of what counts as pantheism and, hence, not consider it as a viable candidate for a pantheistic metaphysics of the divine. This may strike some readers as unduly restrictive.[10]

While some may find it worrisome that accounts like logical pantheism do not receive any attention in what follows, we should consider how the proponents of views like logical pantheism situate their metaphysics of the divine within philosophical theology. What may come as no surprise to some is that Aranyosi is careful to distinguish logical pantheism from what he refers to as "classical pantheism," which identifies God with the cosmos. He explicitly characterizes logical pantheism as a species of *panentheism* on which God *contains* the cosmos.[11] In fact, logical pantheism, according to Aranyosi, "can be considered the most inclusive type of panentheism, because God is identified with Logical Space... ." (Aranyosi 2013, 117). Given Aranyosi's own

---

[10] Similar worries to the ones I am raising with respect to Aranyosi's proposed theory apply to Eric Steinhart's (2004) proposal that a class-theoretic Pythagorean ontology, on which God is identical with the plenum (which is the maximal consistent set), is the best candidate to support pantheism. Two problems arise for this account. First, Steinhart's account countenances abstract entities that are nonnatural in the plenum. Hence, it runs contrary to OntNat. Second, God is more than the cosmos. So it looks more like panentheism. In fact, Steinhart effectively concedes as much by indicating that the plenum is supernatural (Steinhart 2004, 76).

[11] Incidentally, Nikk Effingham's (2021) CaML Model of Pantheism implies that the cosmos is contained by God in some sense (with God constituting the universe but not sharing ontological boundaries with the universe).

admission that logical pantheism is actually a panentheistic metaphysics of the divine we can ignore his proposal and ones like it for the remainder of this exploration of pantheism. (Which is NOT to say that positions like logical pantheism are not deserving of our attention, but any further examination of views like it would go well beyond the scope of this Element.)

Before moving on to clarify some of the relevant concepts for understanding pantheism, there is one more possible worry about OntNat I wish to address. Variants of pantheism have been presented by John Leslie (2001 and 2015) and Yujin Nagasawa (2015) that assume multiverse theory. On multiverse theory, there is not just one universe, but there are potentially infinitely many universes. On Leslie's account, the term "God" can be used to designate either each discrete universe or the entire multiverse (Leslie 2015, 200). On the other hand, on Nagasawa's proposal, if pantheism is true, then God is identical with the entire multiverse (2015, 181). The worry someone may have is that OntNat seems to privilege the universe in which we find ourselves. Hence, multiverse pantheism, which at least *seems* to be naturalistic, is not an ontologically naturalistic metaphysic of divinity.

The worry expressed is misplaced. OntNat is perfectly consistent with multiverse theory because while it identifies what exists with the spacetime world, the spacetime world can be the multiverse or a single universe. In any case, we have either a single spacetime continuum or multiple spacetime continua. If the former is the case, then "the spatiotemporal system" identified by OntNat is a single universe and everything we find therein. If the latter, then it is the multiverse and all that is in it. I will remain silent on whether or not this means that (a) each universe constitutive of the multiverse is a god, (b) the universes are (taken together) God (but none are individually a god), or (c) whether each multiverse is a god who is a part of God.

2.4 Further Distinctions

I have already done some substantial conceptual spadework to get clear on what is meant by "pantheism" when discussing pantheism. In the remainder of this Element, I will assume PAN₃ and OntNat. In this last subsection, I will be focusing on the options for a pantheistic conception of God with respect to how God relates to the constituents of the universe. My remarks about the options will be *mostly* descriptive at this juncture, but I will offer some reasons for why we might find some proposals less satisfying than others.

The first set of distinctions has to do with God's relationship to the spacetime system and the denizens therein. Yitzhak Melamed (2018) has usefully distinguished between two distinct approaches to formulating pantheistic responses to this problem. The first he refers to as "whole-part pantheism" and the second is "substance-mode pantheism" (Melamed 2018, 3–4).

Whole-part pantheism takes the constituents of the universe to be parts of God. According to this view, God is best understood as identical with the mereological sum of the parts of the universe. As understood here, priority pluralism would be an ontological commitment of whole-part pantheism. According to priority pluralism, the parts are ontologically prior to the whole that is the spacetime world. It is not obvious, however, that this view implies that the parts of the spacetime system are ontologically prior to the universe *qua* God for reasons that will, I hope, be clear in a moment. But I think that it will become clear that an ontological commitment of whole-part pantheism is that the parts of God are ontologically prior to God's being. This brings us to a further distinction that Graham Oppy (1997) notes can be made between two versions of whole-part pantheism: *distributive pantheism* and *collective pantheism*. Oppy's distinction echoes a similar distinction made earlier by John Laird in his Gifford Lectures (1941). Laird distinguishes between *distributive pantheism* and *totalitarian pantheism* (1941, 269).

The first version of whole-part pantheism that Oppy identifies is *distributive pantheism*. On distributive pantheism, each thing constitutive of God is divine. This could be owing to an intrinsic property of divinity possessed by each object or owing to how those things stand in relation to other things, with things being said to be divine depending upon how they relate to some other things (Oppy 1997, 321).

One of the most worrisome problems with distributive pantheism is that its proponents appear to commit the fallacy of division. A salient example of the fallacy of division would be if one were to ascribe a kind-attribute to a proper part of some object that is of a particular kind. For instance, if someone were to say that the petrol tank of my car is a car, we would rightly correct that person. It is an *automobile* petrol tank and not a *motorcycle* petrol tank, but that no more makes it an automobile than being a striker on a football team would make one a football team. That each constituent of a football team would be a football team is absurd.

Perhaps the proponent of distributive pantheism is committed to something more innocuous. Suppose we say that, while the totality of existents constitutive of the universe compose God, each proper part is not itself God; but each proper part has the intrinsic property of being divine. This idea strikes me as unhelpful. For one, I worry that the person who might argue this way is assuming that for every predicate we use truthfully in our language we can pick out a property. Many philosophers accept that the proper criterion of ontological commitment is one on which for any true predicate P in the language of some theory, the theory is thereby committed to the existence of Ps. But, on what I take to be a better alternative criterion of ontological commitment, our theories are ontologically committed to whatever must exist in order for sentences in the theory to be true (see Cameron 2008). On this approach, it remains an open question whether a pantheistic metaphysics of the divine is (a) committed to a unique property of divinity and (b) committed to the property in question being possessed by all of the constituents that together compose the divine. And if distributive pantheism is tenable, assuming that the approach I favor to thinking about the ontological commitments of our theories is justifiable, we can apply the predicate "divine" to parts of the universe without having to assume that those parts possess a recherché property of divinity (whatever that would come to). So it could be that neither (a) nor (b) obtain, yet it could still be proper to predicate divinity of the universe and its proper parts.

A more tenable alternative version of whole-part pantheism to distributive pantheism is *collective pantheism*. On this view "the thing of which all things are parts is divine," but the parts need not be (Oppy 1997, 321). This approach strikes me as more promising. For one, it allows us to take the whole (and not its proper parts) to be uniquely picked out as the referent of "God." We can avoid the deeply problematic notion that the proper parts of God are God. But this approach leaves it an open question whether some or all of the proper parts of the universe *qua* God might possess the property of divinity (whatever that might be) or can be truthfully described as divine owing to some truthmakers sufficient for predicating divinity existing. So, endorsing collective pantheism does not close the door on distributive pantheism. Karl Pfeifer (2016) approximates such a view given that he takes "God" to be a mass noun that acts like "gold." Just as "wherever gold is found it is wholly gold, not just part of gold" it is the case that "everything (the whole) is [God] and [God] somehow exists in everything (each of the parts)" (Pfeifer 2016, 43; cf. Laird 1941, 279). We can leave the plausibility of distributive pantheism an open question for further investigation. But, importantly, we can also abandon distributive pantheism while endorsing whole-part pantheism if we can reasonably accept collective pantheism without committing to distributive pantheism at the same time.

The most prominent alternative to any version of whole-part pantheism is substance-mode pantheism. On this approach, there is one substance (e.g. spacetime – see Schaffer 2009) and the things in our experience are modes of the one substance. If you would like, the objects we encounter are collections or bundles of properties of the one substance. This sort of view is most often associated with Baruch Spinoza (see his *Ethics*). Notice that if we accept this view, then God does not possess any proper parts that are objects or substances in their own right. This is because if substance monism is true, then there is only one substance. If there is only one substance, then it lacks substantial parts. If something lacks substantial parts, then it has no proper parts that are substances. It may have spatiotemporal parts, in a loose sense, but these would not be substances (see Heil 2012, Chapter 3). So, for instance, there may be a series of spatiotemporally contiguous regions whose properties are causally connected to one another. But any carving up of spacetime *qua* monistic substance with which God is identical would not track or pick out any substantial parts of God. Rather, they would just be ways we can abstract those parts of the whole in our own minds. So, representing God as any kind of composite object would be a mistake. Rather, God is a simple substance and everything in our experience is a mode of the divine substance's being. I will return to discuss substance monism in Section 4.

My focus in this section has been on clarifying what "pantheism" means and trying to set forth a basic metaphysical picture that can allow us to distinguish it from some other similar accounts of God, such as panentheism. In doing this I have tried to work out some general ontological commitments of a pantheistic metaphysic of the divine that can help us make the aforementioned distinction between pantheism and similar, yet quite different, models of God. No doubt my presentation thus far has been somewhat tendentious and may exclude some models of God that have been assumed to be pantheistic. But I hope that I have offered a principled basis for carving up the conceptual space so we can get beyond some of the confusion that is so common in debates over how we should distinguish pantheism from other accounts of the nature of God, especially panentheism. In any case, some vagueness may be unavoidable here. In the next section, I move to dealing with a topic that is underexplored in the literature on pantheism. Specifically, I will consider what sort of unity the universe must exhibit for pantheistic unity.

3 Kinds of Unity and the Divine Mind

Being told that, on pantheism, God is identical with the totality of existents constitutive of the universe, is not very informative. What is it about that with which God is identical that renders it suitable to describe it as a mind, and a *divine* mind, at that? That people simply have reverential attitudes and experience awe in the face of the vastness of the universe is not a very philosophically satisfying answer to this question. I suggest that at least one desideratum that must be satisfied is that there must be something about the universe as a totality that makes it a fit candidate to describe using theological language. I take it that to satisfy the desideratum in question, the universe must exhibit a certain type of unity we can ascribe to the whole. Specifically, the sort of unity will be the type exhibited by anything that is a fit candidate for describing truthfully as a mind. In this section, I will focus on what sort of unity the universe must exhibit in order to count as a mind.

In what follows in this section, I will survey some different kinds of unity, arguing that the universe must display the sort of unity characteristic of cognitive systems in order to count as a mind. I then consider and respond to some reasons for why one might contend that there is no need to understand the universe as a mind in order for pantheism to be tenable. Finally, I will consider why the sort of unity exhibited by a cognitive system on the scale of the universe would count in favor of understanding the universe as not only a mind, but the *divine* mind.

3.1 What Kind of Unity Is Required for the Universe to Be a Mind?

John Leslie shares my assumption that a pantheistic metaphysics of the divine is one on which the universe can be truthfully represented as a mind. In developing his own pantheistic model of God, Leslie (2001, 43–45) has distinguished between two relevant kinds of unity – structural and existential unity. I will add two more types of unity: minimal unity and cognitive unity. My way of carving out the distinctions will not neatly track Leslie's taxonomy. However, I find much of his thinking on these matters helpful. While the universe must exhibit *cognitive* unity to be the divine mind, other types of unity are no less important. I will proceed by considering minimal unity first. This will be followed by a consideration of structural unity and existential unity. I will spend most of my time working out the details of what must obtain for a system to exhibit cognitive unity.

Regarding minimal unity, Leslie does not use the locution "minimal unity" to describe what I am accounting for here, but the idea seems present in how he writes about structural unity (which I will discuss momentarily). Consider an example Leslie offers: a collection of things that are separate in their existence (Leslie 2001, 44). He gives the example of a collection of stuff in the bed of a truck. Assuming unrestricted composition, such a collection may even compose something. Whatever the case may be about whether they constitute a composite object, the unity exhibited by such a collection is not sufficient for it to be a *system* in any interesting sense. The parts are not integrated in any way and do not answer to any kind of explanations in terms of functions, purposes, or goals. While this kind of unity may be necessary for the constituents of the universe to compose the divine mind, it is clearly not sufficient.

Structural unity is the sort of unity exhibited by any collection of things that exhibits some organization. For Leslie, this sort of unity is exhibited by a heap of stones (Leslie 2001, 44–45). The sort of unity exhibited by the heap of stones is quite minimal. But what all collections that have structural unity have in common, according to Leslie, is that they count as systems. The sense of "system" Leslie has in mind is quite modest. All that he has in mind is that such a collection is organized in some way (Leslie 2001, 44). Clearly, structural unity can come in degrees. Compare a heap of stones to an oak tree. The molecular structure of an oak tree exhibits a kind of systematic unity among its parts that is lacking in the case of the heap of stones. The heap lacks the same degree of structural unity exhibited by the oak tree. The structural unity exhibited by such systems involves elements that are integrated and unified in achieving some sort of *telos*. That end need not have come from outside of the system. But the system as a whole exhibits some sort of purposeful directionality towards various kinds of interactions with various objects. Consider some simple examples. A table's parts are so arranged that it will support objects that have certain features, and an oak tree's parts enable it to behave in ways that are conducive to its survival. Similarly, the members of a hockey team exhibit structural unity as they are organized in a certain way (with different members playing distinct roles) and united for the purposes of achieving the goal of winning games against opposing teams. Like minimal unity, while structural unity may be necessary for the universe to compose the divine mind, structural unity alone is not sufficient (as I hope the preceding examples make clear).

This brings us to existential unity. For Leslie, existential unity is a unity of being. He writes of things united in their existence that they "are in themselves abstractions rather as a brick's length is an abstraction" (Leslie 2001, 45). The whole is prior to the parts. Moving to a cosmic scale, for Leslie, this seems to imply a species of *existence monism*. Existence monists hold that there is only one concrete existent, *the world*. On the version of existence monism defended by Terry Horgan and Matjaz Potrc, the world has no proper parts, but it exhibits a structural richness and is dynamic (2008, 1). They call the world the *blobject* and the ontology that countenances such a view of the world *blobjectivism*. "The *blobject* is objectively real, but lacks any objectively real *parts*" (Horgan and Potrc 2008, 1). Leslie maintains that, if pantheism is true, then ordinary objects in our experience (such as rocks and cats) do not exist separately. They are "patterns inside the divine thinking, which isn't split up between many separately existing thinkers" (Leslie 2001, 44). It is difficult to discern what Leslie has in mind. Specifically, it is unclear whether or not he is committed to a version of existence monism that denies that the world has any spatiotemporal parts that are discrete individual objects. What does seem to be the case is that he is rejecting the notion that existential unity can hold between distinct substances. So, the world seems to lack substantial parts on such a view. Hence, substance monism follows. But this seems too strong a commitment for us if we wish to accept that things exhibit existential unity. In any case, it does not seem to be a necessary condition for existential unity.

Given the implications of Leslie's way of characterizing existential unity, I will characterize existential unity differently. A better, less tendentious, view would allow for it to be an open question whether or not existence monism is correct. A serviceable account of existential unity should allow for other variants of substance monism to remain live possibilities, such as priority monism – on which there is one ontologically basic substance/object that is ontologically prior to its parts (Schaffer 2010, 33). Furthermore, ideally, our account of existential unity should not rule out priority pluralism and other views on which there is a plurality of basic substances. So, it would be optimal for a working account of existential unity to be neutral between existence monism and pluralism as well as between priority monism and priority pluralism.

On my preferred account, things united in their existence will exhibit a degree of structural and functional integration and unity sufficient for them to be truthfully described not only as a discrete system, but also as a system that comprises a whole. More simply, things that exhibit existential unity exhibit a degree of structural unity sufficient for them to count as a single object. The elements of a system that exhibits existential unity can be functionally individuated by their role in the whole. The identity of the elements of systems that exhibit existential unity is determined by the entire system and the role of those elements in the system.

Existential unity on this view would be exhibited not only by artifacts and organisms, but also by ecosystems and even some institutions. Not all of these things are minds or have constituent parts that have minds. So, this account of existential unity is some distance from how Leslie is thinking about it. Importantly, existential unity as I have described it is not sufficient for a unified whole to be a mind (otherwise, every institution or ecosystem will be a mind), but I assume it is a necessary condition.

If pantheism is to provide us with a compelling model of God that is a plausible alternative to other ways of conceiving of God, then the sort of unity exhibited by the universe must be the sort of unity exhibited by systems that we can truthfully describe as *cognitive* systems. What features must a system exhibit in order for it to display cognitive unity? Consider the following schema.

(CU) For any system S, S exhibits cognitive unity if and only if (1) S can be described as a functionally integrated information processor; (2) the processing of information by S, for reasons of S, is directed at producing outputs that may be either an intentional state in S or some purposive behavior of S; (3) the various states of S at any time can be individuated by their functional role in S; and (4) at least some of the different states and processes of S *qua* system must be phenomenally conscious.

Some explanation of each of the elements in this schema is in order.

First, (1) is a standard necessary condition for a system to be a cognitive system on computationalist theories of mind and cognition (CTM). On CTM, all minds can be understood as computing systems. Such systems exhibit a level of functional integration sufficient for cognition. The parts of such a system are involved in a common enterprise of processing information. I assume an account of computing as information processing that is fairly liberal about how to think about information. I am not presupposing, *contra* John Searle (1980), that all information processed in cognitive systems is semantic in nature. Some information processing is nonsemantic. That is, not all computations constitutive of cognition must be individuated by representational content (in particular, they need not be individuated by representational content that is propositional). Gualtiero Piccinini gives the example of "arithmetical calculations carried out on digital computers" (2015, 30). Similarly, some states of and processes within cognitive systems are not representational under any description (think of the process of a signal being transmitted from one neuron to another – the signal itself has semantic content, but the transmission of the signal, which is constitutive of the computational process, does not). Some cognitive processing may involve what Mark Johnston refers to as the direct sampling of the presence of objects, with the content of cognitive states being given to them by "the constitutive modes in which their targets or topics present" (2007, 245). That said, I assume that in many (but not all) cases there is some derived semantic content of such computations (consider the symbols that represent a particular mathematical operation to us) or they are constitutive of computations that involve processing representational states.

Regarding (2), I assume that a genuine cognitive system is not always dependent upon the goal-oriented manipulation of its processing by a third party to produce intentional outcomes. So, for instance, a remote-controlled robot is not a cognitive system. And the reason this is so, is that it does not do what it does for what can be described as *its own* reasons. It does so for the reasons of whomever is controlling the robot. I assume that a unified cognitive system's computational activity is over what Fred Adams and Rebecca Garrison label "*system centered reasons*" (2013, 347). Such reasons that are involved in the information processing of a cognitive system figure in teleological explanations of the system's activity.

That the states of a cognitive system can be individuated by their functional role in the system is the standard orthodox computational view of mental states in the philosophy of mind and cognitive science. (3) simply echoes this commitment. What is important for my purposes here is that nothing about (3) commits us to saying that a description of the functional role of a state of a cognitive system exhausts the nature of the state. I do not wish to suggest that once we know the functional role of a state in a system, we know everything about that state. For my purposes, all that I need is that we can individuate states by the sorts of contributions they make to the unified processing of information in a system like *S*.

Finally, regarding (4), a system that exhibits the sort of cognitive unity I assume we are interested in here must have some phenomenally conscious states and at least some of these states must, together, exhibit phenomenological unity. So, there is something it is like for *S* as a unified system to consciously experience *X* and something it is like for *S* to experience *Y*; and there is something it is like for *S* to experience *X* and *Y*.

The foregoing was, admittedly, quick and no doubt rather superficial. But I believe it will do for my purposes here. What is vital is the following. A system displays cognitive unity if its elements exhibit unified processing of information of the right sort in a particular way and there is something it is like to be that system.

3.2 Do We Really Need Cognitive Unity for Pantheism?

It may be argued that the universe exhibiting the sort of cognitive unity characteristic of minds is not necessary for the truth of pantheism. It may also be argued that the universe's counting as a mind is an untenable hypothesis, reflecting pre-scientific ways of thinking about reality. An example of the second claim at work is found in some remarks by Eric Steinhart (2004). Steinhart asserts the following. "A scientific pantheism cannot affirm that the unity of all things is the unity of life or thought. Such views are relics of seventeenth- and nineteenth-century monisms and idealisms." Steinhart then maintains that the "maximally inclusive unity is a whole of which all other things are parts or a class of which all other things are members" (Steinhart 2004, 77, n. 2). He maintains that other notions of unity are obsolete and that such unity is both "richer" than alternative notions of unity and, unlike them, it is "scientifically viable" (Steinhart 2004, 78, n. 2).

If we ask what we are after with pantheistic unity, it is quickly apparent that the sort of unity Steinhart identifies is inadequate for the task at hand. Levine writes as follows about the sort of unity Steinhart has in mind.

> Attributing Unity on the basis of all-inclusiveness is irrelevant to pantheism. Formal unity can always be attributed to the world on this basis alone. To understand the world as "everything" is to attribute a sense of unity to the world, but there is no reason to suppose this sense of all-inclusiveness is the pantheistically relevant Unity. Similarly, unity as mere numerical, class or categorical unity is irrelevant, since just about anything (and everything) can be "one" or a "unity" in this sense. (Levine 1994, 29)

The universe can have the sort of unity identified by Steinhart and it would make little sense to regard it as divine. If this is right, then the sort of unity Steinhart assumes is sufficient is not obviously richer than any alternatives. If anything, it seems rather anemic and not up to the task of delivering pantheistic unity.

One may concede that a stronger form of unity is needed, but they may still resist the idea that the universe could exhibit the sort of unity characteristic of cognitive systems. Here the worry may come from a shared assumption with Steinhart that the expectation that the universe exhibits any such cognitive unity would not be scientifically viable. But the denial of the scientific viability of the assumption that the universe displays cognitive unity is not obviously war-ranted. For one, there is nothing about hypothesizing that the universe is a mind that is somehow contrary to a scientific worldview. Steinhart's contrary asser-tion fails to be motivated by any appeal to actual work in the sciences that would bar the metaphysical possibility of the universe being a mind. That the universe exhibits a structure similar to what we find with systems that are either identified with minds or taken to provide the ontological basis for minds is an hypothesis that is taken seriously by researchers exploring new boundaries between cos-mology and neuroscience. Preliminary research by Franco Vazza and Alberto Feletti is quite suggestive in this regard. They note that human brains and the universe exhibit "a tantalizing similar morphology." They found that "similar network configurations can emerge from the interaction of entirely different physical processes, resulting in similar levels of complexity and self-organization, despite the dramatic disparity in spatial scales (i.e. $\sim 10^{27}$) of these two systems" (2020, 2 and 7).

Of course, to infer that the universe is a mind or even exhibits a structure similar to the minds with which we are familiar on the basis of Vazza and Feletti's rather preliminary findings would be unjustified. I only mention it to note that the hypothesis that the universe could exhibit the sort of unity characteristic of a mind is not obviously a scientifically untenable notion. Work in the metaphysics of mind often takes up where science leaves us without answers. What is important is that one's hypothesis is consistent with our best science. Nothing about considering whether the universe can exhibit the sort of unity characteristic of a cognitive system is in tension with our best science. If anything, an advantage to the pantheistic conception of God being explored here versus traditional theism is that, at least in principle, a pantheistic account of God presents us with an hypothesis that can, in principle, be confirmed and falsified by scientific evidence. If the universe fails to exhibit the requisite sort of unity and connectivity among its parts sufficient for it to count as a mind, then, at least on the position that I am presenting here, it will fail to deliver the truthmakers to describe it as a divine mind and *ex hypothesi* fail to be God.

Suppose someone is convinced that a stronger version of unity is necessary for pantheistic unity and that the universe's being a mind is a scientifically viable hypothesis that is metaphysically possible. Such a person may hold that while the foregoing is all true, it is not necessary for the universe to exhibit cognitive unity in order for us to have the sort of unity sufficient for the universe to be divine. Existential unity may be enough, according to this interlocutor.

The problem with maintaining that existential unity is enough is that we can have an account of how the universe exhibits existential unity without having anything that even approximates a pantheistic model of *God*. This is not to say that nothing other than God, however God is understood, can be the proper object of religious concern. J. L. Schellenberg has introduced the concept of *ultimism* as a way to understand what is common to all religions. On ultimism, it is the *ultimate* which is the proper object of religious devotion and various religious attitudes such as faith. Such an object of religious concern is "a metaphysically and axiologically ultimate reality (one representing both the deepest fact about the nature of things and the greatest possible value), in relation to which an ultimate good can be attained" (Schellenberg 2009, 1). Schellenberg defines "religion" in terms of such concern for the ultimate as follows. "*S* is religious" means by definition that:

1. *S* takes there to be a reality that is ultimate, in relation to which an ultimate good can be attained.
2. *S*'s ultimate commitment is to the cultivation of dispositions appropriate to this state of affairs. (Schellenberg 2005, 23)

Schellenberg distinguishes between *generic/simple* ultimism and *elaborated/qualified* ultimism (2005, 37–38; 2009, 1–2). Importantly, the *ultimate* (particularly when qualified in terms of *generic/simple ultimism*) is best understood as a placeholder. So, it is not like the *Real* in John Hick's (1989) metaphysics which is the actual object of religious devotion that is represented variously as Brahman, God, Tao, Tien, etc., in world religions. Generic/simple ultimism is just the thesis that there is some kind of metaphysical and axiological ultimate that can be related to in beneficial ways.

While elaborated/qualified ultimism entails generic/simple ultimism, the converse does not hold. Any version of elaborated/qualified ultimism adds "religious content to what it says about ultimates, filling that out in some way" (Schellenberg 2009, 15). Elaborated/qualified ultimism aims to fill in some metaphysical and axiological details. Schellenberg urges accepting generic/simple ultimism for reasons I cannot examine here. What is important for my purposes is that existential unity may be enough for generic/simple ultimism and perhaps some candidate versions of elaborated/qualified ultimism. I maintain that existential unity is not sufficient for pantheism *qua* species of elaborated/qualified ultimism that aims to give an account of the ultimate, where the candidate for the ultimate is understood to be picked out by a model of *God*. Pantheism is thus a species of elaborated/qualified ultimism and, thus, is a more metaphysically demanding conception of the ultimate than we get with generic/simple ultimism or even some other candidate variants of elaborated/qualified ultimism.

Pantheism is contrasted with theism by some (Levine 1994). It should be evident by now that I am not convinced that pantheism should be contrasted with theism *simpliciter* so much as it should be contrasted with traditional theism (and other candidate conceptions of God, such as panentheism). After all, pantheism is making a distinctive identity claim about the universe, namely, that it is identical with *God*. The watershed difference between traditional theism and pantheism does not rest on the question of whether God can be accurately described as personal. After all, there are proponents of models of God found among defenders of both traditional theism and pantheism who take opposing views on whether or not God is personal. (I will return to this issue in Section 5.) The central divide between the pantheist and traditional theist, as I see it, is over how God relates to the world. Any implications for the divine nature will stem from how God relates to the world. That being said, a pantheistic proposal needs to be one that approximates something recognizable as a model of *God*. As such, it seems that the sort of unity we need for pantheistic models to be viable alternatives to traditional theism (and other models of the divine) would be those on which the unity exemplified by the universe is sufficient for it to count as a divine mind. This requires cognitive unity. I take it, then, that any putative account of pantheistic unity that resists understanding the requisite unity as cognitive unity is better described as delivering a species of pan*ultimism* that fails to be a version of pan*theism*.

3.3 Bridging the Gap: Axiology, Divinity, and Cognitive Unity on a Cosmic Scale

If the universe is a cosmic mind, then it is an object that has exceedingly great intrinsic value. Such intrinsic value would be at least one consideration that would render the universe *qua* cosmic mind a proper object of religious devotion and would provide at least some truthmakers for representing the cosmos as the *divine* mind. The relevant source of at least some of the universe's intrinsic value would be its exhibiting the sort of unity characteristic of a cognitive system. At this juncture, it is natural to ask what a metaphysical claim about the unity of the universe has to do with axiological considerations about the intrinsic value of the universe.

In the literature on axiology, there has been some discussion about the intrinsic value of organic unities. Here it may help to distinguish a metaphysical thesis about organic unity that provides the basis for the axiological definition of "organic unity.'

> *Metaphysical:* x is an organic unity $=_{df.}$ x is a collection of diverse objects and their properties that together constitute a unified whole. (see Nozick 1981, 86)

> *Axiological:* x is an organic unity $=_{df.}$ the *intrinsic* value of x is not the same as the sum of the *intrinsic* values of its parts. (Moore 1903, 28)

I assume that the axiological organic unity of a whole supervenes upon its metaphysical organic unity.[12] The metaphysical thesis is not very controversial. But the axiological thesis may be controversial for some. A common simple example may help. On their own, the materials that constitute the discrete proper parts of a work of art may lack intrinsic value. Assume that the whole, *qua* work of art, has significant intrinsic value. If the parts lack intrinsic value and the value of an organic unity were simply the sum of the intrinsic value of its parts, then, assuming the parts lack any intrinsic value, the work of art would also lack intrinsic value. But *ex hypothesi* the work of art has intrinsic value. If this is right and generalizes, then the axiological thesis should not be terribly controversial.

Robert Nozick has argued that the intrinsic value of anything is determined by the degree of organic unity it exhibits (1981, 446). He writes that:

> Holding fixed the degree of unifiedness of the material, the degree of organic unity varies directly with the degree of diversity of the material being unified. Holding fixed the degree of diversity of the material, the degree of organic unity varies directly with the degree of unifiedness . . . in that material.
> (Nozick 1981, 416)

A qualification is in order at this juncture. Nozick notes that the *telos* of an organic unity is "their central unifying factor." Some purposes or ends of some putative unities are ultimately "destructive of organic unity," rendering such unities "disvaluable" and infecting "with disvalue the unity that it animates"

---

[12] Note that I am simply understanding "supervenience" to denote a relation of covariance that does not involve any addition of being. See Heil 1998.

(Nozick 1981, 419). Nozick gives the example of concentration camps, which were highly unified, but were disvaluable owing to their destructive *telos*.

If the organic unity of a whole covaries with its degree of unifiedness as stipulated, we can rank systems by their degree of organic unity. Nozick notes that the kind of organic unity we have with cognitive unity is "an especially tight mode of unification" (Nozick 1981, 417). He goes further, noting that if we were to find cognitive unity on a grand scale (he gives the example of such unity in a planet or a galaxy) "such organically unified entities might be ranked higher in value than an individual human being" (Nozick 1981, 417). I take it that if we find such unity on a cosmic scale, we will at least approximate the upper limit of intrinsic value. This sort of unity is what we would have if the universe exhibited cognitive unity. Even if the *telos* of the system is just the (conscious) processing of information, it would be a *telos* that is not disunifying. But we can go further and take the system to have the realization of life-permitting states of affairs to obtain (which would result in even more organic unity in the universe) to be a *telos* of the cosmic mind (Byerly 2019, 11; cf. Goff 2019). Thus, assuming ontological naturalism (as defined by OntNat), if the universe exhibits the sort of cognitive unity sufficient to count as a cosmic mind, then it would exhibit a very high degree (if not the highest degree that is metaphysically possible) of organic unity. This would be an overall more intrinsically valuable state of affairs than one where the universe lacks such unity.

Why think that an organic unity like a cosmic mind is something that has intrinsic value? I am assuming a fitting attitude theory of intrinsic value. On the approach I favor, we can understand the concept of intrinsic value in terms of the fittingness of certain pro-attitudes towards a state of affairs (Chisholm 1981, 99). A pro-attitude towards a state of affairs p for the sake of p would be appropriate if p is intrinsically valuable – in particular p is something one ought to prefer. In cases of comparative value, if p is intrinsically better than an alternative q, then one ought to prefer p over q (Chisholm 1981, 100). So, if it is fitting to have pro-attitudes towards some state of affairs for its own sake, then it has intrinsic value. We can apply this to organic unities. That we have an organic unity with a *telos* that is not disunifying (and as a matter of fact may increase organic unity in the cosmos) is something that it would be appropriate to prefer, especially over the alternatives. If we have a totality state of affairs with constituents as diverse as what we find in the universe exhibiting the unity sufficient for being a mind, then we have an object that is a fitting object of our pro-attitudes. Hence, it would be something with immense intrinsic value. Therefore, *qua* object of immense intrinsic value, the cosmic mind would be an appropriate object for us to actively value, appreciate, and admire. These would be fitting responses to the totality state of affairs that would obtain if the cosmos were a mind. Going further, the cosmic mind would also be a fitting object of awe and wonderment. Importantly, it is the awe and wonderment one may experience when considering the universe *qua* cosmic mind that is of particular interest.

There is a religious dimension to feelings of awe that has been emphasized, especially in Judaism. Howard Wettstein notes that "there is something *holy* about objects of awe experiences" and adds that it is as if "awe were a faculty for discerning the holy" (1997, 262). Going further, I take it that this sense of awe is the consequence of an encounter with something that can be reasonably and truthfully represented as *divine*.

How do we get from awe to the conclusion that the universe *qua* cosmic mind is a *divine* mind? Levine notes that pantheists take the universe *qua* cosmic unity to be *divine* because the universe is experienced as holy, and, hence, as divine (1994, 48). Levine goes further, noting that "[h]istorically and normatively, the pantheist does not conceptually segregate Unity and divinity" (1994, 49). But is this reasonable?

T. Ryan Byerly has developed an argument for pantheism from the fittingness of the attitude of awe that rests on a *functional claim* and an *objectual claim*. The functional claim is about the function of awe. Byerly maintains that "awe functions in the spiritual domain in the way that admiration does in the moral domain" (2019, 2). Just as admiration is "a fallible guide to the moral domain," awe functions as "a fallible guide to the spiritual domain" (2019, 2). Byerly defines "the divine" as "that for which awe survives critical scrutiny" and "the spiritual life" as "that life that exhibits proper responsiveness to the *divine*" (2019, 2).[13] Awe is, therefore, not just a fitting response to certain states of affairs, but it is a guide to detecting the divine. Byerly writes that "[a]ccording to the awe-based approach to the divine, following the emotion of awe can lead us to detect divine things, the underlying nature of which we can then seek to understand" (2019, 3).

This brings us to Byerly's objectual claim: "the most fitting object of awe is the cosmos" (2019, 6). He writes that "[t]he primary route to affirming this claim is to proceed by identifying the qualities exhibited by objects for which our awe most survives critical scrutiny, and then noting that the cosmos exhibits these qualities *par excellence*" (2019). Byerly argues that the objects that survive critical scrutiny will display two features: *apparently directed complexity* and *beyondness*. With respect to the first (*apparently directed complexity*), the universe displays this to the extent that it produces some

---

[13] It is worth noting that both definitions are compatible with ontological naturalism as defined in OntNat above.

valuable end owing to its complex functioning. If I am right, the relevant complex functioning will be cognitive processing and at least one end to which such processing could be directed would be the realization of conditions that permit the evolution of life. Importantly, while the evolution of life includes a good deal of natural evil, the organic whole still has immense (if not maximal) intrinsic value.

Regarding *beyondness*, Byerly maintains that "[t]he most fitting objects of awe are strictly speaking creatable, though for them to remain objects of awe their creation must outstrip the experient's current powers of creation" (2019, 6). While Byerly offers reasons for accepting this claim, I am not certain that we must accept such a narrow criterion for satisfying beyondness. While I cannot argue for it here, it seems that our awe can be directed at the *power* that can produce certain outcomes. We can be in awe of the powers of the cosmic mind just as much as we might be in awe at the outcomes of the manifestations of those same powers. In either case, what we are in awe of is something that exhibits beyondness in some relevant sense.

By exhibiting the sort of cognitive unity that I am maintaining is required for pantheistic unity the universe will be something that possesses both apparent directed complexity and beyondness. So, if we have reason for thinking that the universe possesses cognitive unity, then the whole that is the universe is not only a cosmic mind, but the *divine* mind.

What I have tried to do in this subsection is provide an axiological bridge between unity and divinity. What I have not explored is whether we can make the move from awe to worship as a fitting response to the cosmos *qua* divine mind. Peter Forrest (2016), Grace Jantzen (1978 and 1984), and Asha Lancaster-Thomas (2020) have all offered arguments for the worship-worthiness of God as characterized by pantheism. But, importantly, they have all built their case up from a *personal pantheist* metaphysics of the divine. On such accounts, it is argued that we have the truthmakers sufficient to truthfully describe God as a person. This is controversial. The debate over whether a pantheistic conception of God is compatible with understanding God as a person will be taken up in Section 5.

For now, I will note that certain practices we associate with worship may still be appropriate even if the pantheistic God is not a person. For instance, William Mander (2007) has argued not only for the propriety of petitionary prayer assuming pantheism, but also for the claim that classical theists cannot make sense of this practice. Importantly, in developing his argument, Mander explicitly disavows personal pantheism. While Mander may be right about petitionary prayer, the broader set of practices we associate with worship may require the further commitment to a conception of God as personal. For instance, Brian

Leftow (2016) has argued against the propriety of worshiping God as characterized by what he refers to as "naturalistic pantheism" – an apersonal conception of deity on which, from what I can tell, God lacks the properties of a divine mind. Such a being would be incapable of being aware or understanding the actions of worshippers and, hence, would not be a proper object of worship, according to Leftow (2016, 71). That said, Leftow explicitly regards personal pantheism as nonnaturalistic (although, assuming OntNat, all of the personal pantheistic accounts of God of which I am aware would count as naturalistic). It may be that nonpersonal variants of pantheism are not vulnerable to Leftow's critique. In any case, even if nonpersonal variants are susceptible to an argument for a pantheistic God not being a fitting object of worship, personal pantheist accounts may be immune to such objections. Whatever the case may be, this is a topic that has not been explored in much depth or detail and is worthy of further consideration.

I will proceed under the assumption that if the universe actually exhibits the sort of cognitive unity sufficient to make it true that the universe is a cosmic mind, then it is also true that it is the divine mind. I will next take up the task of considering whether there is a viable ontological framework that can deliver cognitive unity on a cosmic scale.

4 Unity, Ontology, and the Divine Mind

There has been no shortage of accounts of the unity possessed by the universe sufficient for it to be divine (see Levine 1994 for a survey). But, at least historically, there has not been much of an emphasis on what things must be like in order for the universe to count as the divine *mind*. I take it that the most promising path to take in exploring pantheistic unity will be to consider whether there is an ontological framework that can provide us with the metaphysical tools for ascribing to the universe the sort of unity exhibited by a cognitive system. In this section, the focus will chiefly be on some of our ontological options that might deliver the desired kind of cognitive unity.

I will consider four contemporary approaches that I assume are consistent with ontological naturalism: substance monism, ontic pancomputationalism, panpsychism, and, finally, an approach that is best described as panprotopsychist that appeals to an ontology of powers to explain cognitive unity. I favor the last of these approaches.

4.1 Can Substance Monism Deliver the Requisite Type of Unity?

On substance monism, there is one irreducible substance in the world. I assume, first, that a genuine substance is an object that is a property bearer. Second, the properties that characterize a substance are modes or ways a substance is. Finally, genuine substances are simple. They lack substantial parts – that is, they have no parts that are themselves substances. A substance may have spatiotemporal parts, but if we have a complex object that has substantial parts, then it is not a substance (see Heil 2012, Chapters 2 and 3).

A candidate object for being the one substance that was proposed by Spinoza is the universe, which he simply refers to as "nature." He identifies God with nature in the preface and Proposition 4 of Part IV of his *Ethics*. Spinoza makes this same explicit identification of God with nature in a letter to Henry Oldenburg penned in April of 1662. He writes: "I do not separate God from nature as everyone known to me has done" (1662/1985, 188). Edwin Curley (1969) has argued that the identification of God with nature is not with nature *simpliciter* (i.e. the universe) but rather with *Natura naturans*. *Natura naturans* picks out "what is in itself and is conceived through itself, *or* such attributes of substance as express an eternal and infinite essence, i.e. . . ., God, insofar as he is considered a free cause" (Spinoza 1677/1985, E1p29, 434). *Natura naturans* is contrasted with *Natura naturata*, which Spinoza identifies with "whatever follows from the necessity of God's nature." These are "modes of God's attributes insofar as they are considered as things which are in God, and can neither be nor be conceived without God" (Spinoza 1677/1985, E1p29, 434). The modes in question are the finite particular things in our experience (see E1p25).

Against Curley's interpretation, Yitzhak Melamed argues that "Spinoza leaves no doubt that he takes finite modes to be God in some sense or respect" (2013, 18). Evidence for this is found in the same part of the *Ethics* where Spinoza introduces the distinction between *Natura naturans* and *Natura naturata*. He writes that "[T]he modes of the divine nature have also followed from it necessarily and not contingently (by P16) – either insofar as the divine nature is considered absolutely (by P21) or insofar as it is considered to be determined to act in a certain way (by P28)" (1677/1985, E1p29, 433). Finite modes of God are no less divine for being finite. If this is right, assuming that God is identical with nature, then God is identical with nature *simpliciter*. There is only one substance, which is a thinking substance under a description and an extended substance under another description (Spinoza 1677/1985, E2p7, 451).

Substance monism has few adherents today. C. B. Martin (2007, Chapter 16) has argued for substance monism, contending that "[a] propertied space-time is a one object universe and space-time satisfies the correct definitions of 'substratum'" (195). But the most forceful recent defense of substance monism has been offered by Jonathan Schaffer (2009). Schaffer defends monistic substantivalism, which holds that spacetime is the only substance and the objects in our experiences are propertied perduring spacetime regions.

There are at least four ways to think about the relationship between spacetime regions and objects in our experience given monistic substantivalism (Schaffer 2009, 134). The first is the *unrestricted identity view*, according to which every spacetime region or collection of spacetime regions is a material object. The unrestricted identity view stands in contrast to the *restricted identity view*, which holds that spacetime regions that satisfy some further criterion (e.g. maximal connectedness) are identified with material objects. The third and fourth views take objects to be constituted by, rather than identical with, spacetime regions. Like the identity versions, they differ on whether composition is restricted or not. The *unrestricted constitution view* takes every spacetime region to constitute a material object. The *restricted constitution view* requires that spacetime regions satisfy some further condition in order to count as objects.

The substance-mode pantheist who appeals to substance monism to account for how the universe can exhibit the sort of unity sufficient for cognitive unity and, hence, to be truthfully described as a divine mind is not free to pick from any of the four versions of monistic substantivalism. This is because we need an account of how things are structured in the world to provide us with the truth-makers for representing the universe as a mind. Unrestricted composition will not help us here. We need an account of how things are arranged that will exhibit existential unity as I described it above. It is not obvious that we can get even structural unity if we allow for things to combine haphazardly. But if we have restricted composition, it seems there needs to be something about spatiotemporal regions and their properties that restrict their combining in ways that will deliver the sort of unity the pantheist is after. I will return to this worry in subsections 4.3 and 4.4. For now, I will just note that we need something to act as the ontological glue, so to speak, that will allow us to treat certain combinations of things as exhibiting existential unity, counting as entities in their own right.

If, with Spinoza, we hold that God is infinite and simple, then God is ontologically prior to finite things. Thus, the substance monist view will commit us to priority monism. An ontological upshot is the rejection of whole-part pantheism. Moreover, while contemporary priority monists talk of the whole being ontologically prior to its parts (see Schaffer 2010), the Spinozistic pantheist will insist that the contemporary priority monist is making a category mistake, especially if by "parts" the priority monist is allowing that the universe has *substantial proper parts*. God-nature is a simple substance. So, the universe lacks any proper parts. Now if by "parts" we simply mean "spatiotemporal parts," then there is nothing objectionable to representing the whole that is God *qua* substance as being ontologically prior to God's parts. Particular things are *in* God, not parts of God (Melamed 2013, 48). Notice that a logical consequence of this is that, while we may truthfully describe individual things as divine, they are not themselves God or gods. They are *modes* of God. So, a strong form of distributive pantheism is ruled out.

Can substance monism deliver what we need for the universe to be unified in the right way to count as the divine mind? If the question is whether substance monism alone will deliver the unity we are after, we must answer in the negative. But if the question is whether or not a suitably embellished substance monist view can deliver cognitive unity, then I am more hopeful. Supposing we embellish the account, one may then be justifiably worried about exactly what work *substance monism* is doing for us. In other words, if substance monism does not, on its own, explain the existential and cognitive unity of the universe that delivers the truthmakers for representing the universe as a mind, then substance monism is not an ontological commitment of pantheism. We may have further, independent reasons for being substance monists, but it is not clear that endorsing pantheism gives us such a reason.

The Spinozistic substance monist may point out that the one substance is indivisible, and this provides a starting point for the unity necessary. But, at most, this gives us a kind of existential unity of the whole. That the universe exhibits existential unity is not sufficient for it to possess cognitive unity. An appeal may then be made to *Natura naturans* and the governing principles of the universe as supplying this. But we need to know what it is about *Natura naturans* that will deliver the right kind of unity. And, again, it is not clear that getting the story right demands accepting substance monism. So, while there may be independent reasons for accepting substance monism, it is not clear that endorsing it will deliver what we are after when we are thinking about the unity of the universe *qua* divine mind. Therefore, the pantheist is free to reject substance monism. Thus, I suggest we turn our attention elsewhere for an account of cognitive unity.

4.2 The Universe as a Computational System

Pancomputationalism hypothesizes that all physical systems perform computations (Piccinini 2015, 51). We can further distinguish between some variants of pancomputationalism. *Unlimited* pancomputationalism states that "every sufficiently complex system implements a large number of non-equivalent computations" (Piccinini 2015, 51–52). *Limited* pancomputationalism is the thesis that every physical system performs *a* computation "or perhaps a limited number of equivalent computations" (Piccinini 2015, 54). *Ontic* pancomputationalism goes further and takes the universe to be a computational system. Moreover, ontic pancomputationalism is committed to the further claim that everything in the universe is also a computing system (or part of one) (Piccinini 2015, 56).

Ontic pancomputationalism is usually wedded to a version of limited computationalism. Konrad Zuse (1982) and Edward Fredkin (2003) are often identified as its progenitors. The universe is represented variously as a cellular automaton, a universal Turing machine, or a quantum computer (Pexton 2015, 302).

While no analytic philosophers who have written on pantheism have appealed to ontic pancomputationalism explicitly, Eric Steinhart (2004) has approximated this view by arguing that a Pythagorean ontology is best suited to satisfy various desiderata of a pantheistic conception of the divine. I will not address Steinhart's arguments directly below. That said, the problems I will present for ontic pancomputationalism will be problems for Steinhart's theory, especially since the problems for ontic pancomputationalism will stem from a version of Pythagoreanism being one of its ontological commitments. The similarities end there. Recall from subsection 3.2 that Steinhart denies that the universe is best understood as the divine mind. I have offered reasons for why it is best to proceed under the assumption that a tenable version of pantheism will be committed to cognitive unity being the sort of unity that the universe must display. So, as provocative and interesting as Steinhart's proposal is, I shall ignore it for my purposes.

The argument from ontic pancomputationalism to the universe being a mind is quite simple. Suppose that the computational theory of mind (CTM) is right. On CTM, all cognition is computational, but not all computational activity is cognitive activity. So, minds are computing systems, but not all computing systems are minds. Suppose that ontic pancomputationalism is true. One may then reason as follows.

1. Minds are computing systems. (CTM)
2. The universe is a computing system. (Ontic Pancomputationalism)
3. So, (1) and (2). (from (1) and (2))
4. If (1) and (2), then the universe is a mind.
5. So, the universe is a mind. (from (3) and (4))

While the foregoing is a valid argument, it is not obviously sound. Even if we assume pancomputationalism, we need to establish that the universe can be the right sort of computing system to count as a cognitive system. Not every computing system is a cognitive system. They may all be protocognitive, but they are not all clearly cognitive *simpliciter*. Ergo, we need to clarify the commitments of pancomputationalism and consider whether we have reason to accept premise (2). Moreover, and perhaps more importantly, we need to determine whether, assuming that the conjunction of (1) and (2) is true, we have good reasons to think that the universe is a mind (and hence that the consequent of (4) is true). I will argue that, even if we assume the truth of computationalism about cognition (and, hence, the truth of premise (1)) and we assume ontic pancomputationalism, the conjunction of these two theses does not provide us with sufficient reasons to accept that the universe is a mind. So, assuming the truth of the antecedent of premise (4), we lack adequate reasons on the basis of ontic pancomputationalism alone to accept the truth of the consequent. Hence, the truth of premise (4) is in doubt. I will consider premises (2) and (4), in that order.

Regarding premise (2), mapping accounts of what makes a system a computational system can easily deliver the conclusion that the universe is a computational system. Piccinini notes that, on a simple mapping account, any physical system S performs some computation C if:

(i)   There is a mapping from the states ascribed to S [or some subset thereof] by a microphysical description to the states defined by computational description C, such that:

(ii) The state transitions between the microphysical states mirror the state transitions between the computational states. (Piccinini 2015, 17).

We can render a simple mapping account more complex by restricting what counts as an acceptable mapping by strengthening clause (ii). This can be done by, for instance, requiring that the microphysical transitions either support certain counterfactuals, demanding that the microphysical state transitions be causal, or that the system manifests a disposition it possesses to transition from one state to another (Piccinini 2015, 19–20). It is easy to see how, if disposition-ascriptions are made true by the causal powers of objects constitutive of a system, the dispositional account implies the causal account and, in turn, gives an account of the truthmakers for the relevant counterfactuals (it would be true that <If S were in p, then S would q> given that S is disposed to q when in p). The relationship between these varied approaches is unimportant for our purposes here. For now, what is important is that so long as a system can satisfy (i) and (ii) (even if restricted), we will get at least some version of limited computationalism. There will be mappings between computational descriptions and physical systems. It is a short step from this to the claim that the entire system that is the physical universe is a computational system.

I will not devote any space to considering some of the objections to mapping accounts that focus on how they lack the resources to distinguish between computational explanations and computational models (Piccinini 2015, 23).

While these issues are of particular importance for determining the viability of mapping accounts for understanding computational processing and, further, cognitive processing, they will not be of concern here since these are matters that will take us too far afield. The limitations of pancomputationalism for the purposes of thinking about the metaphysics of pantheism will stem from other problems. For now, it is worth stopping to consider how ontic pancomputationalism could provide a picture of the universe as exhibiting the sort of continuity and unity needed to be a mind.

The version of ontic pancomputationalism that best delivers the sort of continuity and unity needed is one according to which the universe is a quantum computer (see Lloyd 2006). The term "bit" is used to denote both some smallest unit of information and the physical system that represents that information (Lloyd 2010, 46). We can represent these bits of information as zeros and ones. Classical computers will process the bits of information as discrete units. A quantum computer will process quantum bits of information – variously referred to as "qbits," "qubits," and "qudits." Such a computer inherits the weirdness of quantum mechanics. For instance, a qubit in a state of super-position will be in two states simultaneously. So, its state will be represented not by a 0 or a 1, but by both simultaneously. Importantly, a collection of qubits can manifest quantum entanglement. The universe, on the quantum version of ontic pancomputationalism, is a quantum computer that manipulates qubits (Piccinini 2015, 57). Continuity is a real feature of the cosmos owing to the quantum entanglement of qubits. We can model and explain the behavior of the universe in terms of computations it performs.

The foregoing was all very quick. For now, I only wish to note that we at least have some *prima facie* reasons for accepting premise (2) of the argument. As we will see, however, there will be metaphysical reasons for thinking that no *ultima facie* case can be made for premise (2) (at least not without amending the account).

Turning now to premise (4), it states something a bit stronger than what ontic pancomputationalism states. It says that if minds are computing systems and the universe is a computing system, then the universe is a mind. But while it may be correct that all minds are computing systems, it does not follow that all computing systems are minds. Even if we assume that all computing systems are protocognitive, in some sense, it does not follow that just because a system is a computing system that it is a cognitive system. If we suppose that the universe is a computing system that satisfies all of the relevant information-processing desiderata associated with being a cognitive system that are specified in the CTM, it may still be the case that the system lacks anything like phenomenal consciousness. This is so because phenomenal consciousness resists being characterized computationally (see Chalmers 1995). So, the universe could be a computing system, exhibiting the sort of unity of such a system, while failing to be a mind. Perhaps from ontic pancomputationalism we get that the universe can be truthfully represented as a protomind, but we need more to justify that it can be truthfully described as a mind. But I think there are metaphysical reasons for being skeptical of ontic pancomputationalism being able to deliver any such story, at least not without some ontological emendations. The chief worry is that some version of Pythagoreanism is an ontological commitment of ontic pan-computationalism. Why this is worrisome will require some explanation.

On ontic pancomputationalism, any physical system, including the universe, is a system of computational states. Piccinini notes that this implies that "[c]omputation is ontologically prior to physical processes" (2015, 58). Differently stated, things "bottom out" ontologically in information (in the physical sense). There are two options here. One is to take computations to be configurations of physical stuff (such as fundamental physical objects and their properties). But this option would seem to imply that the physical stuff provides the truthmakers for representing physical systems computationally or else as providing the ontological grounds for computational processing. Such an approach would make physical processes ontologically prior to computation, which would reverse the order of ontological priority endorsed by the ontic pancomputationalist. One way to put the ontic pancomputationalist's position is thusly: Software is ontologically prior to hardware. What is ontologically basic are computations, which are abstracta, mathematical entities that have no spatiotemporal location and no causal powers (Piccinini 2015, 58). Such an ontological reduction of the physical to the mathematical is a version of Pythagoreanism. In this case, rather than a Pythagoreanism on which all is just numbers or sets, we have a computational Pythagoreanism on which all is computation (and physical systems are aspects of such computations) (Piccinini 2015, 58–59).

If we suppose that there are abstracta, that they would constitute everything physical would be deeply problematic for at least two reasons (see Martin 2007, Chapter 6). First, physical things have causal powers and do things in space and time. On the other hand, abstract entities have no spatiotemporal location or causal powers. As Piccinini notes, "it is not clear how abstract entities that have no causal powers and no spatiotemporal location can give rise to concrete things that exert causal powers through spacetime" (2015, 59). Second, physical objects have categorical properties – concrete qualities such as mass, charge, spin, shape, etc. Abstracta lack concrete qualities (Piccinini 2015, 59). Why is any of this a problem? Recall that we are sorting through our ontological options for providing the basis for understanding the universe as a mind. Minds are things that do stuff and, importantly, have qualitative states – there is something it is like to be a thing that has a mind. Abstracta are not well-suited to provide the basis for the sort of cognitive unity we are after.

In concluding this subsection, I should be clear about what I am NOT claiming. I do not wish to suggest that we cannot accurately represent the universe as a computational system. While ontic pancomputationalism may be a view that we ought to reject, it is only because of its ontological commitment to taking everything to be reducible to computations. But if we say, whatever the universe is made of, that its states and its processes can be modeled and even explained computationally, then I do not think there is anything objectionable to any such pancomputationalist view. A mapping account of computation can deliver the goods if divorced from ontic pancomputationalism and wed to an ontology that can provide us with what we are after if trying to account for how the universe can be a mind. I will consider two more alternatives that I think are promising candidates.

4.3 Panpsychism and the Divine Mind

In recent years, some authors have argued that a panpsychist framework can deliver the requisite sort of unity for the universe to count as a mind. In brief, "panpsychism" denotes the metaphysical hypothesis that postulates that phenomenality is ubiquitous in the universe (Nagasawa 2020, 259). Some recent defenders of pantheistic models of God have taken some version of panpsychism to be an ontological commitment of pantheism. For instance, John Leslie argues that "pantheism is the theory that being real inside [the divine] mind is the only reality that our universe has" (2001, 18). He goes further, noting that "the structures of physical objects are structures in the divine mind, the structure of divine experiences" (Leslie 2001, 93). But, for Leslie, while he maintains that his pantheistic metaphysics of the divine entails panpsychism, the variant of panpsychism he assumes is one on which everything has the extrinsic property of there being consciousness of it but not the intrinsic property of being conscious (Leslie 2001, 93). I assume this means that while not everything is a subject with experiences, everything is experienced by a subject, namely, the divine mind.

Leslie's view on these matters can be usefully compared and contrasted with those of another recent defender of pantheism, T. L. S. Sprigge. Sprigge's pantheistic account of the divine is explicitly committed to an idealist version of panpsychism. Everything is experience, according to Sprigge (2006, 484). He maintains that "only a panpsychist view of the world … can cope with the two facts (1) that only experience exists and (2) that the physical world exists"

(Sprigge 2006, 484). The ontological framework he offers is then applied to God, whom Sprigge identifies as "the Absolute" or "the Eternal Consciousness" (Sprigge 2006, 487). While Leslie identifies his view as a species of panpsychism on which everything is experienced, Sprigge advances a version of panpsychism on which everything just is experience and is composed of streams of experience. While Leslie holds that the things that populate the cosmos would not exist "in the total absence of consciousness," he explicitly denies that "stars, planets[,] and water molecules are themselves conscious" (2001, 93). Sprigge, on the other hand, holds that every finite thing that populates our universe is itself a distinct finite stream of experience that is "a component in one divine eternal consciousness" (2006, 487).

Their differences notwithstanding, both Leslie and Sprigge appear to endorse versions of *constitutive cosmopsychism*. Constitutive cosmopsychism weds a version of priority monism to constitutive panpsychism. Some discussion of each of these and the proposals to which they stand in contrast is in order before turning to whether any type of panpsychist proposal can help us account for how the universe can exhibit the unity and qualities sufficient for it to count as a mind.

Panpsychist proposals can be understood as variants of either micropsychism or cosmopsychism.[14] Micropsychism is a smallist version of panpsychism on which micro-level objects have phenomenal properties. Following David Chalmers, I will refer to these properties as "microphenomenal properties" (2017a, 24). Microphenomenal properties can be contrasted with macrophenomenal properties, which are properties that characterize "what it is like to be humans and other macroscopic entities" (Chalmers 2017a, 24). The micropsychist holds that macrophenomenal properties are ontologically dependent upon microphenomenal properties. Differently stated, macroexperience is ontologically dependent upon microexperience.

A divide exists between two types of micropsychists. On the one hand, there are *constitutive micropsychists*, and, on the other, *emergent micropsychists*.

Constitutive micropsychists hold that macroexperience and the macrophenomenal properties constitutive of those experiences are grounded in/derived from/realized by/constituted by microexperiences and the microphenomenal properties constitutive of those experiences (henceforth, I will simply use "constituted" to pick out the general variety of ontological dependence relation that holds between macro-level entities and the micro-level entities upon which

---

[14] What I am identifying with the term "micropsychism" others simply identify with panpsychism, contrasting panpsychism with cosmopsychism. Following Goff (2017a, 173), I take micropsychism to be the standard approach to panpsychism, but cosmopsychism is no less panpsychist given that both approaches affirm that phenomenality is ubiquitous.

they depend). As Chalmers puts it, "constitutive [micropsychism] holds that microexperiences somehow add up to yield macroexperience" (2017a, 25). Macrophenomenal properties and the experiences of which they are constitutive are not ontologically fundamental or basic, they are, for lack of a better way of putting it, the aggregate sum of a combination of microphenomenal experiences and their constitutive properties. They are complex properties.

Emergent micropsychists deny that macroexperiences are constituted by microexperiences. Rather, they are themselves ontologically fundamental, being strongly emergent from microexperiences. So, while macroexperiences and macroproperties are ontologically dependent upon microexperiences and microproperties, there is no "constitutive connection" between the former and the latter (Chalmers 2017a, 25).

Cosmopsychism stands in contrast to all versions of micropsychism. Proponents of cosmopsychism hold that "phenomenality is everywhere throughout the cosmos because the cosmos as a whole is phenomenal" (Nagasawa 2020, 262). We can distinguish between three very general versions of cosmopsychism: *existence cosmopsychism*, *priority cosmopsychism*, and *constitutive cosmopsychism*.

Existence cosmopsychism is structurally parallel to existence monism. Just as existence monism holds that only one object exists, existence cosmopsychism is committed to there being "exactly one consciousness, the cosmic consciousness" (Nagasawa and Wager 2017, 117).[15]

Priority cosmopsychism is structurally parallel to priority monism. Just as priority monism holds that there is one ontologically fundamental object, "priority cosmopsychism says that exactly one basic consciousness, the cosmic consciousness, exists" (Nagasawa and Wager 2017, 116). Analogous to priority monism's commitment to the concrete objects in our everyday experience existing derivatively, priority cosmopsychism takes all of the particular, discrete consciousnesses of humans and other animals (and whatever else might be conscious) to be derived from the cosmic consciousness (Nagasawa and Wager 2017, 117).

Both existence cosmopsychism and priority cosmopsychism are silent on whether monism (specifically, existence monism and priority monism) is an ontological commitment of either of them. Yujin Nagasawa and Khai Wager maintain that they are independent, arguing that "priority cosmopsychism does not rely on priority monism" (2017, 117). And they remain neutral on whether or not priority monism and priority cosmopsychism are compatible.

---

[15] Existence cosmopsychism is defended in Jaskolla and Buck 2012.

Unlike existence cosmopsychism and priority cosmopsychism, *constitutive cosmopsychism* is ontologically committed to priority monism. Philip Goff (2017a) has developed and defended constitutive cosmopsychism, taking it to result from wedding priority monism to constitutive panpsychism. I mentioned constitutive micropsychism above. Constitutive panpsychism, as a general hypothesis, will assert that the consciousness of humans and other animals is constituted by some more fundamental kind of consciousness. A version of priority monism is assumed on which "the universe is a fundamental unified whole, and all other material entities are aspects of that whole" (Goff 2017a, 234). The consciousness of subjects such as humans and other animals is grounded by subsumption in the whole, which is itself "a fundamental unified [conscious] subject" (Goff 2017a, 234). Regarding grounding by subsumption, Goff offers the following conditions for one entity to ground another by subsumption:

> Entity X grounds by subsumption entity Y if (i) X grounds Y, and (ii) X is a unity of which Y is an aspect. (Goff 2017a, 221)

An example of grounding by subsumption would be the following. Suppose that property-instances are ways that objects are. The object is a unified entity whose existence grounds the ways that it is. Turning to states of affairs involving discrete conscious subjects, the discrete conscious subjects, in virtue of being grounded by subsumption in the universe, "are aspects of states of affairs of the universe having such and such states of [consciousness]" (Goff 2017a, 234).

Before exploring whether any variant of panpsychism can provide us with the tools we need to get an account of how the universe can exhibit cognitive unity, it is worth saying a bit about a common set of ontological assumptions endorsed by many current proponents of panpsychism. Taking this brief detour is important given that these ontological assumptions will bear on the tenability of panpsychist proposals.

Regarding the nature of objects and their properties, many panpsychists endorse a version of Russellian monism. Russellian monism is a species of ontological monism that is in agreement with physicalism that there is one kind of stuff that is identified by physics. Where Russellian monism parts company with standard physicalist views is in its denial that physics tells us the complete story about the nature of what there is.

On Russellian monism, "the phenomenal and the physical are deeply intertwined" (Alter and Nagasawa 2015, 422). Three core commitments are shared by most versions of Russellian monism (Alter and Pereboom 2019). These are (a) *structuralism about physics*, (b) *realism about quiddities*, and (c) *quidditism about consciousness*.

Regarding (a), *structuralism about physics*, physics tells us about "the relational structure of matter but not its intrinsic nature" (Chalmers 2017a, 26). Hence, Russellian monists maintain that (a) is not the complete story.

Enter (b): *realism about quiddities*. Most versions of Russellian monism assume that the dispositions of the entities described in physics have a purely categorical base consisting of *quiddities* (which are purely categorical/qualitative properties whose essence is divorced from any causal role they have). Quidditism stands in contrast to *dispositional essentialism*. Dispositional essentialism is the view of properties on which they have a dispositional essence. Quidditism amounts to a rejection of dispositional essentialism and an endorsement of the notion that the identity of a basic property is independent of its causal role or dispositional profile. Fundamental properties are purely categorical/qualitative. The fundamental intrinsic nature of objects and their properties is noncausal and nonmodal. Owing to this, "there may be two possible worlds that are exactly alike with respect to causal facts, but which differ in which properties play which causal roles" (Wang 2016, 172). The dispositional essentialist would reject this claim. They would hold that any two worlds that are exactly alike with respect to causal facts will be exactly alike with respect to which properties play which causal roles.

Finally, most Russellian monists endorse (c) *quidditism about consciousness*. On this view, some quiddities are "microphenomenal properties" (Chalmers 2017a, 26).

I will focus on just two versions of constitutive Russellian panpsychism in my discussion about whether panpsychism can deliver cosmic cognitive unity: *constitutive Russellian micropsychism* and *constitutive Russellian cosmopsychism*. In the next two subsections I will take up the prospects of accepting each of these, in turn, for getting an account of the universe as a mind.

4.3.1 Constitutive Russellian Micropsychism and Pantheism

On this approach, the universe *qua* mind would possess macrophenomenal properties that are constituted by microphenomenal properties. This sort of view can be wed to an understanding of the universe as a computational system (divorced from the ontological assumption of ontic pancomputationalism) to deliver an account of the universe as a mind. Thus, any macroexperience of the universe is constituted by microexperiences which are themselves constitutive of the computational processes that make up the cognitive life of the cosmic mind.

On any panpsychist account of the cosmic mind (whether micropsychist or cosmopsychist), the experiences of discrete centers of consciousness (such as distinct human persons, nonhuman animals, etc.) can be understood as thoughts in the cosmic mind.[16] More specifically, they would implement structures that partially constitute the cosmic mind. If we follow John Leslie, we could go further, identifying the systems that have consciousness with thoughts in the cosmic mind (2001, 8). So not only would the thoughts of my cat and me be thoughts within the cosmic mind, but *we* would also both be thoughts in the cosmic mind. This sort of view need not imply something as radical as a version of idealism on which the material world is an illusion. Leslie writes that "You ought surely to continue counting yourself not only as real, but as a real material thing" (2001, 8). Thus, Leslie seems to be in agreement with the constitutive Russellian panpsychist (both the micropsychist and the cosmopsychist), allowing that the objects we encounter either have properties that are at once both physical and phenomenal or are neither but provide the truthmakers for phenomenal and physical descriptions. (Recall from my discussion of Leslie above that material objects have the relational property of being experienced.)

It may be instructive to contrast the implications of making the claim that we are thoughts in the cosmic mind assuming some version of panpsychism with what a similar claim would imply on traditional theism. If traditional theism is correct, then the divine mind is not identified with the physical universe. Thus, if we assume traditional theism and make the claim that the material objects we encounter are thoughts in the divine mind, then we would be denying their reality as material objects (Leslie 2001, 8). But assuming panpsychism about the cosmic mind (and that God is identical with the cosmic mind), then we do not have the same implication for the status of material objects.

Assuming constitutive Russellian micropsychism, material objects would constitute the thoughts of the divine mind much as states of a human brain would constitute the thoughts of a human mind. The mental life of the universe *qua* cosmic mind would be ontologically grounded in these thoughts. But the mental life of the cosmic mind would not be exhausted by these discrete thoughts. The entire cosmos would exhibit a unity of consciousness. Just as the conscious experiences of animals like ourselves exhibit a unity, the cosmic mind would exhibit unified experiences. But the cosmic mind, like our minds which would be constitutive of it, could think discrete thoughts and focus on those thoughts that would be proper parts of the larger experience. Of course, what it would be like to have a unified conscious experience *qua* cosmic mind is difficult to grasp. That said, the challenge posed is no different in kind from similar challenges of knowing what it would be like to have experiences we have never had.

---

[16] Another alternative is that they are like so many holes in the divine mind (see Forrest 2007 and 2016b). I discuss this sort of view in subsection 4.4.

The basic idea before us is, at first glance, a coherent one. Micro-objects have microphenomenal properties that combine and are integrated to deliver macro-phenomenal experiences in macro-level objects, with the übermacro-object being the cosmic mind. But there are reasons to be concerned about the viability of this sort of proposal. I will focus on just two problems. The first comes from Yujin Nagasawa (2020), who has argued that the metaphysics of the divine that we will get if we assume a panpsychist view like constitutive Russellian micropsychism will commit us to a species of polytheism. The second problem is over how microexperiences can combine to yield macroexperiences.

4.3.1.1 Micropsychism and Polytheism

Micropsychism may not be up to the task of delivering an account of the whole universe as a *single* unified divine mind. In a survey piece exploring the relationship between panpsychism and pantheism, Nagasawa has argued that micropsychism (which he designates by the term "panpsychism" – which is contrasted with cosmopsychism) and pantheism are not structurally parallel and are, in fact, "radically distinct metaphysical views" (2020, 260).

Nagasawa defines pantheism as follows:

> Pantheism: Divinity is everywhere throughout the cosmos. (2020, 260)

"Panpsychism" is defined by Nagasawa as follows:

> Panpsychism: Phenomenality is everywhere throughout the cosmos. (2020, 259)

Nagasawa argues that while the two definitions express similar claims, what each one means by "x is everywhere throughout the cosmos" is quite different (2020, 260). He writes that:

> Panpsychism says that phenomenality is everywhere throughout the cosmos because *everything in the cosmos* is phenomenal. On the other hand, pantheism says that divinity is everywhere throughout the cosmos because *the cosmos as a whole* is divine. In other words, while the focus of panpsychism is on individual things in the cosmos the focus of pantheism is on the cosmos as an entity in its own right. Panpsychism says that phenomenality is immanent and pantheism says that divinity is immanent but they reach these conclusions from different directions – indeed from the exact opposite directions. (Nagasawa 2020, 260)

Note that the thought here is that micropsychism is making a claim about the universe owing to the nature of the particular constituents of the universe while pantheism, as Nagasawa characterizes it, is making a claim about the ubiquity of divinity in the universe owing to the whole being divine.

Nagasawa maintains that while pantheism and micropsychism are not parallel, polytheism and micropsychism *are* parallel. The parallel to micropsychism would be the claim that "[d]ivinity is everywhere throughout the cosmos because *everything in the cosmos* is divine." Nagasawa asserts that "this is an extreme form of polytheism" (2020, 261). He notes that the immediate challenge to this sort of view is that if we say that the individual parts of the universe are divine and maintain that from this claim we can derive the divinity of the whole, then we risk committing the fallacy of composition (2020, 264). But he allows that, if we add certain assumptions, we can get the entailment of pantheism from polytheism, and vice versa, thereby avoiding the fallacies of composition and division. Nagasawa writes that:

> In order to show that polytheism and pantheism are compatible, we can add an extra assumption that the cosmos as a whole is divine *in virtue of everything in the cosmos being divine*. Here, the divinity of individual things in the cosmos is ontologically prior to the divinity of the cosmos as a whole. (2020, 264)

Nagasawa distinguishes this sort of "bottom-up approach" that "starts with the divinity of individual things in the cosmos . . . [deriving] the divinity of the whole from it" from a "top-down approach." On a top-down approach, the parts of the cosmos would be divine in virtue of the whole being divine. So "the divinity of the cosmos as a whole is . . . ontologically prior to the divinity of individual things in the cosmos" (Nagasawa 2020, 264). I mentioned both possibilities in subsection 2.4. This bottom-up proposal was articulated by John Laird, but never explored in any detail (1941, 279). Like Laird, Nagasawa does not develop this account. So, its ultimate success is an open question.

Two observations are in order. First, Nagasawa is right that micropsychism and polytheism make parallel claims. But it seems like an open question whether micropsychism can deliver a version of pantheism on which the whole universe comprises a system that exhibits cognitive unity. Assuming success in showing that a coherent metaphysics of the cosmic mind can be provided based on micropsychist assumptions, the most reasonable position to accept about the cosmic mind *qua* divine *might* be a version of distributive pantheism. But I have my doubts. If it is shown that the universe could be a mind, our interest is in the *whole*. Having a whole that is a mind made of parts that possess phenomenal qualities from which it inherits its consciousness is not quite the same as having a whole that can be described as divine whose parts somehow inherit being divine from the whole. As mentioned in subsection 2.4, such a move amounts to committing the fallacy of division. We need independent reasons to move from micropsychism to the universe being a mind, and then to its being a divine mind, and, finally, to the parts being divine. I am skeptical about the success of any such project, but limitations of space will not allow me to consider what such a line of reasoning might look like and what problems, if any, it will face.

This brings me to my second observation. The central challenge to the micropsychist does not come so much from polytheism as much as from a more general problem with any sort of micropsychist strategy to explain consciousness. In brief, the more central challenge has to do with whether constitutive Russellian micropsychism can give us the resources needed to account for how the universe can count as a mind that has unified conscious experiences.

4.3.1.2 The Combination Problem

When considering what problems a constitutive Russellian micropsychist account of the cosmic mind will face, readers familiar with the literature on panpsychism in the philosophy of mind will no doubt immediately think of the combination problem. In brief, the combination problem can be expressed as a question: "How do microexperiences combine to yield macroexperiences?" (Chalmers 2017a, 36).

The combination problem for the divine mind may be more acute than the challenge posed by accounting for the conscious experiences of medium-sized cognizers such as humans and other animals. When we move to the cosmic level, not only do we need to worry about how the experiences of the constitutive elements of systems such as human organisms combine to give us the sort of unified conscious experiences we have, but we also need an account of how the discrete centers of consciousness that are individual humans and other animals can combine with each other and with the various other constituents of the physical universe to generate a cognitive system with unified conscious experiences.

The combination problem was first identified by William James (1890/1950) and named by William Seager (1995). David Chalmers (2017b, 185–191) distinguishes seven different arguments that express different variants of the combination problem. Success in responding to one of these arguments does not guarantee success in responding to the others. I will only focus on *the subject-summing problem* given limitations of space and since it has received considerable attention. The problem is over how myriad microsubjects of conscious experiences can be combined to yield a macrosubject of conscious experiences. Following Chalmers, the argument for the subject-summing problem can be represented as follows (2017b, 186).

(1) If constitutive [Russellian micropsychism] is true, the existence of a number of microsubjects with certain experiences necessitates the existence of a distinct macrosubject.

(2) It is never the case that the existence of a number of subjects with certain experiences necessitates the existence of a distinct subject.

---

(3) Constitutive [Russellian micropsychism] is false.

If one accepts micropsychism and is trying to make sense of how pantheism can account for how the universe can exhibit cognitive unity, the combination problem and the problem of unity are really just two expressions of the same challenge.

In her discussion of micropsychism and pantheism, Joanna Leidenhag (2019) expresses skepticism about whether any version of pantheism that attempts to account for the unity of the cosmos based on micropsychist assumptions can be successful. This is owing at least in part to the challenge posed by the subject-summing version of the combination problem. Whether or not Leidenhag's skepticism is well-placed depends upon whether certain proposed solutions will work. I will briefly consider one response to the subject-summing version of the combination problem with the goal of ascertaining whether constitutive Russellian micropsychism can deliver not only an account of the unified consciousness of medium-sized macrosubjects, but also the divine mind.

Consider the following thesis:

> *Metaphysical Isolation of Subjects* – For any group of subjects, instantiating certain conscious states, it is possible that just those subjects with those states exist in the absence of any further subject. (Goff 2017b, 292)

The foregoing thesis (which, following Goff, I will refer to as MIS) is equivalent to the second premise in Chalmers' version of the subject-summing argument and is a premise in an argument Goff takes to represent the sort of reasoning that will lead one to reject the tenability of micropsychism owing to the combination problem. There is no need to present that argument here. Goff denies that there is good reason to accept the truth of MIS. He grants that it follows from MIS that "subjects of experience cannot sum merely in virtue of their existing." But he denies that it rules out "the possibility of there being some state of affairs of certain subjects of experience *being related in some specific way* which necessitates the existence of some distinct subject of experience" (2017b, 292).

The phenomenal bonding relation bonds "subjects together to produce other subjects of experience" (Goff 2017b, 292). Goff admits that we do not have a clear conception of what such a relation would be like, but he maintains that this is not surprising given that our epistemic situation is such that the focus of the sciences is on the world's "mathematico-causal structure" while "the phenomenal bonding relation is not a mathematico-causal relation" (2017b, 292). The epistemic problem he identifies is owing to a species of the *structural mismatch problem* (a variant of the combination problem). In brief, the problem is that the subjective structure of our phenomenally conscious experiences does not match the objective structure of their neural correlates (see Lockwood 1989, 16). Goff expresses this problem concisely when he notes that "If you examine my brain, you will not be able to see it instantiating phenomenal properties" (2017b, 293). He goes further, asserting that an implication of this is that given that we can only know via introspection what it is like to be a single subject of experience, we cannot know what it is like to "experience subjects of experience qua subjects of experience as related." Thus, we lack the ability to "form a transparent conception of the phenomenal bonding relation" (2017b, 293).

With Goff, I propose referring to the problem of determining the conditions under which "subjects combine to produce a further subject" as the *special phenomenal composition question* (2017b, 296). There are three options Goff considers. The first is *restricted phenomenal composition*, according to which "some but not all subjects are such that they bear the phenomenal bonding relation to each other" (2017b, 296). Goff takes this to be the commonsense answer to how a plurality of discrete subjects can compose a unified subject. Proponents of this approach might take it to be the case that "[p]articles form a conscious subject when and only when they form an organism" (2017b, 297). But this answer is not promising owing to vagueness in the boundaries between cases where entities count as organic versus nonorganic. Such vagueness is evident in what Goff calls "'organic borderline cases' – cases where there is no fact of the matter as to whether or not we have a human organism – at the beginning and end of an organism's existence" (2017b, 297). Moreover, he notes that the organism criterion for being a conscious subject would exclude nonorganic systems from being conscious. But there is no obvious reason that would justify such an exclusion. Owing to considerations such as this, Goff recommends rejecting restricted phenomenal composition.

We are left with two options in response to the special phenomenal composition question if Goff is right. On the one hand, we can embrace *nihilism*, according to which no subjects bear the phenomenal bonding relation to one another. The other alternative, which is Goff's preferred response, is *unrestricted phenomenal composition*, according to which "for any group of subjects, say, the particles forming your nose, my teeth, and the planet Venus, those subjects are related by the phenomenal bonding relation and hence produce a further subject" (2017b, 296). The phenomenal bonding relation on this view is just the spatial relation between objects. Thus, "for any group of material objects, the members of that group, being spatially related, constitute a conscious subject" (2017b, 299). He asserts that this approach delivers a richer conception of the spatial relation "that goes beyond the mathematical conception of it we get from physics" (2017b, 300). The deep story about the spatial relation is that it is the phenomenal bonding relation. The upshot is a rather radical conclusion: "the only intrinsic determinable is consciousness, the only relational determinable is phenomenal bonding" (2017b, 300).

If Goff is right, then there is something it is like to be the collection of particles that form my teeth, my nose, and the planet Venus. But that the combination of those things composes an object that is conscious strains credulity. While it is a putative solution to the combination problem, it fails to deliver the goods we need to account for the unity of our conscious experiences. There being a unique subject of experiences hardly seems accounted for by the possibility of the fusion of the particles that constitute my ventral striatum, my son's lollipop, and the beer in my refrigerator composing a discrete object. If anything, I am personally left scratching my head wondering how this is helpful in getting us to understand how subjects can combine to compose a subject with a unified first-person perspective. In particular, it only raises more questions about why my own experiences as a subject do not include so much more than what I experience *qua* embodied. And if the value of this approach is questionable when considering the conscious subjects with whom we are most familiar, it is not obvious that this can help us understand how the universe can be the divine mind. But perhaps the problem will diminish if we shift away from constitutive Russellian micropsychism and adopt constitutive Russellian *cosmopsychism*.

4.3.2 Constitutive Russellian Cosmopsychism and Pantheism

Goff has developed and defended a version of constitutive Russellian cosmopsychism (2017a). I will focus my attention here on how he extends his theory to develop an *agentive-cosmopsychist* account of the cosmic mind. I will not consider the applications of the account that he explores. Rather, my chief focus will be on whether it can deliver an account of unity sufficient for understanding the universe as the divine mind.

I will not restate the commitments of constitutive Russellian cosmopsychism (henceforth, I will just refer to it as "cosmopsychism'). But Goff notes that cosmopsychism alone does not entail pantheism or anything close to it. He writes that

> We need not think of the universe as a supremely intelligent rational agent. Intelligence and agency are characteristics of highly evolved conscious

creatures, which the universe is not. It is more plausible that the consciousness of the universe is simply a mess. It may be hard for us to *imagine* a single mental state involving such wildly conflicting contents, but I see no reason to think that such a thing is impossible. (Goff 2017a, 243)

Given what Goff says about phenomenal bonding, that the universe would be something of a disunified mess should not be very surprising. Goff's claim about the entailments of cosmopsychism should allow us to see why a mere commitment to cosmopsychism will not deliver cosmic cognitive unity. So, what more is needed?

For Goff, the apparent addendum to the basic cosmopsychist picture is the assumption that the universe is a conscious *agent* that responds to reasons and has "a basic disposition to form spontaneous mental representations of the complete future consequences of all of the choices available to it" (2019, 111). Notice that if the universe is a conscious agent as described by Goff, then it must exhibit cognitive unity. Goff maintains that "everything that happens is determined by the rational choices of the universe," which is constrained by the laws of physics that "record the limitations of the universe's capacity to act" (2019, 109). Goff takes this capacity to be basic and says little more beyond this, which is somewhat frustrating. It is frustrating, in part, because it is natural for one to ask the following: In virtue of *what* can we truthfully describe the universe as having this capacity for responding to reasons as well as the capacity for representing the consequences of possible choices?

Goff's answer to the worry at hand seems to amount to his asserting that the capacities in question are ontologically basic (2019, 109 and 112). But even if they are ontologically basic and not grounded in some other features of the universe, we need to know more about these capacities and why the sort of disunified mental life that the universe would have on cosmopsychism as presented by Goff would have such capacities.

Goff appeals to the explanatory utility of positing agentive cosmopsychism to explain the fine-tuning of the universe, arguing that this approach has advantages over the multiverse hypothesis. But while I think that Goff is right that agentive cosmopsychism is better positioned to account for the fine-tuning of the universe, we need a more complete metaphysical picture of why it is reasonable to expect the universe to be a cosmic agent. Importantly, if the universe is a cosmic agent, then it is a cosmic mind. And if it is a mind, then it must display the sort of cognitive unity that minds have. It seems that positing agentive cosmopsychism, absent a further metaphysical story about the origins of the cognitive unity of the universe, will fail to deliver what we are after.

Given the lack of a proper metaphysical story about how the universe can possess cognitive unity, we are still stuck with the combination problem. Given Goff's commitment to unrestricted phenomenal bonding, the universe is a phenomenological mess. And, while Goff assumes priority monism, as noted earlier, priority monism alone cannot deliver what we are after if we wish to have a solution to the combination problem. But there are other worries.

The combination problem gets most of the attention in both the literature critiquing panpsychism and in the defenses offered by its proponents. What gets relatively little attention is the division/individuation problem. Suppose that, assuming cosmopsychism, we have an account of how the entire universe can exhibit cognitive unity. We are now faced with the following question: "How do cosmo-experiences divide to yield the unified macroexperiences of discrete subjects?" Leidenhag identifies six variants of this worry. It is the sixth version of the question that strikes me as most salient given that, from what we have thus far, we are no closer to a solution to the combination problem.

> How does the cosmically structured (we might say sparsely structured), unbounded cosmic consciousness or field of experience structure itself in such a way as to hold within it distinct (compactly structured) subjects and qualities? (the Structural Individuation Problem). (Leidenhag 2019, 551)

I do not know how the cosmopsychist can avoid this worry without modifying some of their ontological assumptions.

The main culprit behind both the combination and individuation problems is the commitment to quidditism by many who endorse versions of constitutive Russellian panpsychism (whether micropsychism or cosmopsychism). Recall that, if we assume quidditism, the causal and modal profile of a property is not essential to its identity. That things combine or are divided in one way rather than another is a brute fact. Assuming quidditism about properties, "the property that exercises the charge role in the actual world can exercise the mass role in another possible world" (Esfeld 2012, 160). So, assuming quidditism, we cannot argue that microphenomenal properties are essentially such that they are directed at reciprocal manifestations that have being combined or divided into unified macroexperiences as an outcome.

Owing to the commitment of standard statements of constitutive Russellian panpsychism to quidditism, it is hard to avoid the conclusion that "no set of conscious subjects necessitates the existence of a further conscious subject" (Chalmers 2017a, 36). So, nothing about the nature of the relevant microphenomenal properties alone can help us explain how they combine to yield derivative macrophenomenal properties such as we would get from a complex system with unified conscious experiences.

4.4 A Powers-based Solution

Some philosophers have built upon a powers ontology to make sense of pantheistic unity (see Bauer 2019, Buckareff 2019, and Pfeifer 2016). The accounts offered by these authors may best be characterized as panprotopsychist solutions that rest on a panintentionalist thesis that results from the presupposed account of properties. By "panprotopsychism" I mean the metaphysical hypothesis that "fundamental physical entities are protoconscious." Further, on such accounts, the properties of fundamental physical entities are not phenomenal but they "can collectively constitute phenomenal properties, perhaps when arranged in the right structure" (Chalmers 2017a, 31). It is in virtue of the properties of objects being powers that they can exhibit the structure requisite for cognitive unity.[17]

The version of the powers-based approach that holds the most promise is one in which all of the intrinsic properties of objects are powerful qualities.[18] On this sort of account, the powers of objects are not grounded in/realized by some categorical properties. Rather, on this view, there may be a conceptual distinction between the dispositional/powerful and the categorical/qualitative, but this distinction is only a *conceptual* distinction and not an ontological distinction. There is no "ontological division which the conceptual distinction maps" (Mumford 1998, 145; see also Heil 2020, 21). Powers and qualities are the same thing, albeit under different descriptions.

Recall the three ontological assumptions that are shared by both constitutive Russellian micropsychism and cosmopsychism: (a) *structuralism about physics*, (b) *realism about quiddities*, and (c) *quidditism about consciousness*. I have argued that the combination and individuation problems for panpsychist accounts of pantheistic unity stem in part from a commitment to properties as quiddities. Proponents of a powers-based account of cosmic cognitive unity can accept (a) while rejecting (b) and (c). Importantly, the proponent of this strategy can agree that physics does not tell us the whole story about the nature of fundamental objects and their properties. They can agree with the Russellian monist that properties have a categorical/qualitative essence. But, contra the Russellian monist, the powers-realist will insist that the essences of fundamental properties are not just categorical (so they can grant that (b) and (c) approximate the truth about properties, but that (a) also tells us something about them). The dispositional/dynamic/structural story we get from physics

---

[17] If one assumes that the powers in question are phenomenal properties, one can endorse a full-blooded panpsychist solution built up from a powers ontology. But none of the proposals to date have appealed to properties understood as *phenomenal* powers (see Mørch 2020).

[18] For defenses of this view, see Heil 2003 and 2012; Jacobs 2011; Martin 2007; and Mumford 1998.

also tells us something about the essences of properties. Their causal and modal profiles are essential to their identities.

Powerful qualities *qua* powers are directed at manifestations with other powers that serve as reciprocal manifestation partners. We can describe powers as "for" or "about" various manifestations with other powers. Following C. B. Martin, I will refer to each manifestation a power is for as a "disposition-line" of the power (2007, 29). The disposition-lines of powers provide us with the truthmakers for claims about what is metaphysically possible (see Borghini and Williams 2008). So, for instance, if it is true that it is possible for some sodium bicarbonate to neutralize a quantity of hydrochloric acid, the truthmakers for this sort of claim would be the actual powers of the sodium bicarbonate and hydrochloric acid and the manifestations at which they are directed when partnered.

The directedness of properties *qua* powers is the distinguishing feature of properties that proponents of powers-based solutions to the pantheistic problem of unity make an appeal. In particular, owing both to the directionality of powerful qualities and their qualitative nature, such accounts can deliver the truthmakers for describing objects as exhibiting intentionality and can provide us with the ingredients of phenomenal consciousness.[19] I will focus on some of the core, shared features, of these proposals. That said, the account I sketch should be understood as my own, even if it shares some common features with other powers-based solutions to the problem of pantheistic unity.

Regarding powers and intentionality, all objects exhibit intentionality of some form owing to the directionality of their powers. Something exhibits intentionality to the extent that it is (1) about, for, or directed at something; (2) directed at things that are present or may not be present; and (3) may exhibit indeterminacy with respect to that to which it is directed (with its reference fixed by context). I will consider each of these in turn.

As mentioned above, the properties of objects are directed at various manifestations with the properties of different objects with which they might interact in a causal process. For instance, a power of a chemical compound is directed at producing certain outcomes in combination with the powers of another chemical compound. Hence, owing to the assumed *directionality* of all properties on this theory, we get a sort of *aboutness* to powers that is characteristic of intentionality (Martin 2007, 59; Molnar 2003, 63).

---

[19] It may come as no surprise to those familiar with debates about phenomenal consciousness in the philosophy of mind that the sort of proposal I will offer will be built upon intentionalist/representationalist assumptions about phenomenal consciousness coupled with the ontology of properties as powerful qualities.

The powers of objects include "a capacity to project to the non-existent," which is the second mark of intentionality mentioned above (Heil 2003, 221). What powers are directed at are not always things that exist in their environment. For instance, what the causal powers of a chemical compound are directed at can exist or not exist. Even if there were no hydrochloric acid in this part of our universe, sodium bicarbonate would still be directed at neutralizing it.

Finally, regarding the third mark of intentionality mentioned, powers can also be determinate or indeterminate with respect to their directionality (Martin 2007, 59; Molnar 2003, 64). Consider the following example from C. B. Martin. A hen has the power to lay an egg and, depending upon the context, has the power to lay a particular egg (Martin 2007, 59). Similarly, a chemical compound can have a property directed at a general sort of manifestation with a certain type of property of another compound (for instance, the solubility of sodium chloride is directed at dissolving when it is partnered with the power of dihydrogen oxide to dissolve sodium chloride). And the same power can be directed at a specific manifestation with a specified token manifestation partner (the power of *this* portion of sodium chloride partnering with the power of *that* dihydrogen oxide).

In virtue of the directedness of their powers, we can accurately describe the most fundamental simple substances (and complex objects composed of these substances) as exhibiting a very basic kind of intentionality. The intentionality of our mental lives is, of course, robust, while the sort of protomental physical intentionality exhibited by the powers of a chemical compound is minimal and evidently not sufficient on its own for the complex intentionality exhibited by systems that count as cognitive systems. But the ingredients of mentality are in the basic stuff in the world.

The foregoing remarks about intentionality and protomentality have been quick. Intentionality is only half of the story. If intentionality were the whole story about mentality, while we would have the ingredients we need for thought and, hence, cognitive processing, we would be missing an account of what it is like *to be* a particular cognitive system.

To fill out the story, we have to consider properties *qua* qualities. As qualities, properties of objects can be arranged in such a way to be experienced as collections by systems with the power to apprehend qualities. On the account I am assuming, the apprehension of qualities would be the outcome of a causal process involving manifestations of properties *qua* powers (which are *directed* at those manifestations). A cognitive system's unified conscious experience is owing to the system exhibiting an appropriate level of integration in the causal processes constitutive of information processing that is owing to how that system's properties *qua* powerful qualities are arranged and interacting with one another.[20] Subjective experiences are the outcomes of such causal processes.

An upshot of the powers-based solution is that composition is restricted. In particular, what sorts of things can combine is restricted by disposition-lines of the structural powers of the objects (Marmodoro 2017, 121–122). And composite objects will exhibit a sort of unity we would not find in arbitrarily combined conglomerates of objects whose properties are not directed at combining in the ways characteristic of the integrated complex substances we encounter. Importantly, both the functional and phenomenal unity exhibited by conscious cognitive systems like the minds of animals such as humans is owing to the form imparted to them by the powerful qualities directed at combining in a way sufficient for mentality.

I hope that the sketch just offered can allow readers to see a way forward in our thinking about pantheistic unity provided by a powers ontology. This approach suggests a way to dissolve the combination and division problems identified above. We avoid these problems for two reasons. First, we avoid the problem of division given that a metaphysics of properties as powerful qualities entails that composition is restricted. Second, given that the view under consideration does not take experiences to be fundamental, we do not have the combination problem faced by panpsychist proposals. I will briefly discuss each of these in reverse order

First, regarding the problem of division, if the fundamental properties are quiddities, we have no basis for individuating discrete macroexperiences in such a way that we have discrete experiences with boundaries that are necessarily fixed in a certain way owing to the properties of objects. Recall that, on Goff's account, the phenomenal bonding relation obtains in virtue of a spatial relation holding. On the powers-realist account, we can individuate various cognitive systems that are parts of the larger cognitive system that is the divine mind. Each such constitutive cognitive system would be a discrete cognitive unity whose boundaries are fixed by the bodies of agents whose constitutive powers are directed at the requisite functional integration to constitute discrete centers of cognitive processing and consciousness. So just like the processing of a single neuron is not the same as the processing of another, we have discrete cognitive processing in each cognitive system that is constitutive of the divine mind. But these systems together with the larger processing of information around them are like the constituents of a neural network. Together, they are active elements in the processing of information at the cosmic scale.

---

[20] Readers familiar with integrated information theory (IIT) in consciousness studies will recognize the similarities between what I am proposing and IIT. This is not an accident. For more on IIT, see Tononi and Koch 2015.

What about the combination problem? On the view on offer, there are no microexperiences. But we have macroexperiences that would, presumably, be part of a larger cosmic-macroexperience. The computational processing that is characteristic of a cosmic cognitive system would involve the integrated processing of information by discrete processing units. Each conscious cognitive system that is constitutive of the divine mind would be a discrete unit of cognitive processing that together would process information on a larger cosmic scale. The experiences of each unit would be combined on a cosmic level. Here Goff's phenomenal bonding as a spatial relation would be sensible. But now we have the powerful qualities that give rise to discrete experiences interacting with the larger cognitive system that is the divine mind. Here it may help to model conscious divine cognition as related to the conscious cognitive activity of discrete systems as a sort of metacognitive processing involving second-order consciousness of first-order conscious states. So, God would have conscious knowledge *de se* of the contents of the minds of each discrete cognitive system, but it would be meta-level rather than object-level conscious divine cognitive activity.

The foregoing can be coupled with the Swiss-Cheese Theory of persons and the divine that has been offered by Peter Forrest (2007 and 2016b). On Forrest's account, which he christened "Qualified Personal Pantheism," "human and similar minds are not parts of God but rather they are like holes in God, who is identical [with] the rest of the Universe" (2016, 22). In earlier work, he identified the holes as being filled by our consciousness and agency (2007, 28). In recent correspondence, he elaborated on the account, noting that "every substance is part of God, but not every entity, because the free decisions of creatures and associated mental states are the 'holes.'" He added the following:

> I now hold that where there are two or more agents with prima facie power over a region, the one that has the greater unity has the greater power in that region. This results in the paradoxical power of creatures, because we have greater unity than God in the region of our brain-states represented to us as a body-image.[21]

The powerful qualities view of properties can deliver the sort of picture of the divine mind Forrest prefers. Consider an individual noncosmic mind. The powers constitutive of that mind are more tightly integrated in that location than the complete constellation of powers of the cosmic mind. The powers of a discrete agent are directed at manifestations that are constitutive of cognitive processing and conscious episodes within that system. The powers of such cognitive systems may be directed at manifestations that result in larger

---

[21] From email correspondence on 1 July 2021.

cognitive processing or conscious episodes of the cosmic mind, but these subsystems may be relatively autonomous vis-á-vis the cosmic mind. Notice that the organisms in question would still be proper parts of the universe. But the consciousness and cognitive processing that goes on within such organisms would be discrete processes and experiences from one another and from the divine mind (even if their processing and outputs may figure in the cosmic-level cognitive processing).

I have not settled any issues here about what sort of ontological picture can deliver the sort of cognitive unity I have argued we need to have in order to have a sufficiently strong version of pantheistic unity. Some candidates appear to be more promising than others. My hope is that future work will explore ways we might combine some of these alternatives. I fully expect more accounts to be offered. This seems like the topic in the metaphysics of pantheism that demands the most attention given (a) how little attention it has received compared to other issues and (b) the general lack of ontological seriousness of many existing proposals. That said, I am hopeful that we will see progress on this topic in the years to come, especially if interest in pantheism on the part of analytic philosophers of religion increases.

5 Personal or Impersonal Pantheism?

It is widely assumed by many working in analytic philosophy of religion that pantheism is committed to rejecting any conception of God understood as a person. For instance, Levine is representative of this perspective. He treats the denial of divine personhood as a defining point of departure of most variants of pantheism from traditional theism. Levine maintains that most pantheists are committed to denying that "God is a person or anything like a person" (1994, 3). Levine asserts that "there appears to be no *prima facie* case for attributing personality to the pantheistic deity, and plenty of reason to reject it" (1994, 148). But recent years have witnessed some growing interest in developing versions of personal pantheism.[22] And some traditional theists have taken up the cause of denying that God is a person.[23] So that this is a watershed issue in current analytic philosophy of religion that divides pantheism from traditional theism seems wide of the mark.

In this section, I will briefly consider why some have insisted that pantheism is committed to a nonpersonal conception of God and present reasons for why we might endorse a personal pantheistic conception of God. While I accept the

---

[22] See, for instance, Coleman 2019, Forrest 2016, Jantzen 1984, Lancaster-Thomas 2020, and Pfeifer 2016.

[23] See, for example, Davies 2016, Hewitt 2019, and Thatcher 1985.

coherence of a suitably qualified personal pantheism, I do not think that a conception of God as personal is an ontological or conceptual commitment of pantheism any more than it is an ontological or conceptual commitment of traditional theism. In the remainder of this section, I will first articulate some criteria for counting as a person. I will then articulate and offer responses to three arguments against the pantheistic God counting as a person. My goal is simply to show that personal pantheism is not obviously incoherent and may be a live option for those attracted to pantheism to accept.

5.1 What Are the Criteria for Personhood?

In what follows, I will proceed under the assumption that any distinction that may be drawn between being a *person* versus a *personal being* does not track anything metaphysically deep.[24] So in offering criteria for personhood I should be understood to be offering criteria for being a personal being.

An obviously inadequate definition of "person" is the following:

(P1) S is a person $=_{df} S$ has a mind.

The problem with (P1) is that lots of things have minds that we do not identify as persons. For instance, my cats have minds. I realize that this is controversial for some substance dualists and those who think that humans are the only organisms with minds. I will ignore such perspectives given that they either stem from ignorance of the scientific evidence for the rich cognitive lives of nonhuman animals or they are based on mistaken beliefs about human uniqueness that are somehow irrefutable by scientific evidence. So, I take it that a system that displays cognitive unity can fail to be a person.

So, if my cats have minds, why do they fail to count as persons? They fail to count as persons owing to their failing to have certain mental capacities and powers. So, a better definition of "person" is the following.

(P2) S is a person $=_{df} S$ has a mind that possesses certain capacities and powers.

What are the relevant powers required for personhood?

A candidate necessary condition for personhood that I will assume is the capacity for having a first-person perspective.[25] Regarding what is characteristic of the first-person perspective, Lynne Rudder Baker writes that it "is a *perspective* because it is a view on reality from a particular orientation; it is *first personal* because the orientation is from the subject's own point of view" (2013, 128). She further distinguishes between what she calls a "rudimentary" and a "robust" first-person perspective. Someone has a *rudimentary* first-person

---

[24] See Page 2019 for a critique of attempts at articulating accounts of God as a personal nonperson by classical theists.

[25] Baker (2013, 176ff) takes the capacity in question to be an irreducible dispositional property/power.

perspective if they are the mere subject of *conscious* experiences. Someone has a *robust* first-person perspective if they are the subject of *self-conscious* experiences. A normal human infant is an example of someone with a rudimentary first-person perspective, while a normal adult human is an example of someone with a robust first-person perspective. One difference in the human case is the acquisition of language. Baker writes:

> A creature with only a rudimentary first-person perspective has the capacity to interact – intentionally and consciously – with things in the immediate environment. Lacking language, however, a creature with only a rudimentary first-person perspective (human or not) is unable to refer to herself at all, by means of "I" or a third-person description. Nevertheless, a rudimentary first-person perspective situates an entity in an environment, located at the origin of its perceptions. All the mental activities of a creature with only a rudimentary first-person perspective are, by default, first-personal.
>
> (Baker 2013, 128–129)

A robust first-person perspective, on the other hand, requires a self-concept.

> To have a robust first-person perspective, one must be able to manifest it. To manifest a robust first-person perspective, one must be able to consciously conceive of oneself as oneself*, to be aware that it is oneself qua oneself that one is conceiving of. That is, one must have a self-concept. The thought that one would express by saying "I wish that I* were a movie star" contains the concepts, *wish, movie, star*, and one's self-concept. (Baker 2013, 135)

Baker argues that the first-person perspective is a vital component to understanding some of the other capacities of persons, including rationality and intentional agency. I will ignore any of the other capacities given that they are not obviously as important for an account of what must be true for someone to count as a person.

I will assume that the rationality condition includes the capacity to evaluate and respond to reasons, understood as considerations that weigh for and against one's accepting the truth of a statement (theoretical reasons) or for and against one's acting in a certain way (practical reasons). The intentional agency condition is just the capacity to exercise purposeful agency by acting or omitting to act for reasons, being guided by an intention that represents a plan for one's achieving some goal.

Given the foregoing, I will assume the correctness of the following schema:

> S is a person if and only if (i) S has the capacity for having a robust first-person perspective, (ii) S has the capacity to evaluate and respond to reasons (both theoretical and practical), and (iii) S has the capacity for exercising agency in pursuit of goals represented in plans.

All three of these capacities would be possessed by systems with a high level of cognitive unity, representing robust capacities for common types of information processing (about oneself, how one relates to one's environment, what one should believe/accept, and what one should do and how to do things in pursuit of a goal). Coupled with having a robust first-person perspective, which involves the manifestation of a capacity for self-consciousness, we get a picture of those things that count as persons as exhibiting a high degree of cognitive unity. In what remains of this section, I will consider three objections to understanding the pantheistic God as satisfying these criteria for personhood.

5.2 Consciousness, Pantheism, and Personhood

Sam Coleman has argued that the central version of the problem of personhood for pantheism stems from worries about whether the universe can be conscious. In brief, the thought is that the following three statements comprise an inconsistent triad (Coleman 2019, 89).

1. God is a person.
2. God is the universe.
3. The universe is not a person.

Given (2) and (3), (1) must be false. If we insist on the truth of (1), coupled with (3), we get the denial of (2). Coleman observes that "the most important reason that surfaces among [critics of personal pantheism] is the thesis that persons are essentially conscious entities, and the universe, taken as the manifest image conceives of it, is not, as a whole, conscious" (2019, 90).

Coleman denies that personhood requires consciousness and offers a panqualityist solution to the problem of divine personhood for pantheists. He maintains that persons are identified with "suitably integrated sets of intrinsically non-conscious qualities, such as to form a mind" (2019, 93). He takes these qualities to be "of the broad kind we meet in consciousness" (e.g. "sensory, emotional, and cognitive qualities") (2019, 90–91). These qualities are constitutive of persons, even when a person is not conscious of them. Moreover, the person may not be capable of being conscious at all. "Personhood is merely revealed by, not dependent upon, consciousness" (2019, 93). If that is the case, then the universe can be a person despite lacking consciousness (2019, 91).

Coleman allows that "the universe . . . is deeply and surprisingly causally and constitutively connected," noting how quantum field theory supports this idea (2019, 93). The person of God spans "the great mass of non-conscious qualities that . . . *form* the physical universe by providing its categorical base" (2019, 93). But God is not conscious on Coleman's view. While he notes that "[our] persons exist in God's person," along with everything else that constitutes the universe, it seems he only allows for brains to be conscious. But why think this? If any system exhibits the same sort of structural and functional integration as a brain that is capable of consciousness, then, assuming panqualityism, why think that it cannot have conscious experiences? I have maintained that the sort of cognitive unity we want for pantheism involves there being something it is like to be God. My worry is that Coleman is assuming that, because we cannot access what it would be like to be the universe, there must be nothing it is like to be the universe. But this problem, of course, generalizes to brains and the behavior of systems with brains (recall the structural mismatch problem mentioned in subsection 4.3.1.2). Nothing about what I observe gets me any closer to knowing what it is like to be any other cognitive system.

If we take having a first-person perspective (even a rudimentary one) to be essential to being a person, then God is not a person assuming Coleman's solution. A way around this is to allow that God has the *capacity* to be conscious (and even self-conscious) while allowing that God's consciousness may not always be manifested uniformly throughout the universe. Moreover, there is nothing incoherent about the stronger view on which the divine capacity for consciousness is always manifested to the same degree in the cosmos. Precisely how such a story would go is a matter to be taken up elsewhere. That said, I will quickly note that, even if God has the capacity for consciousness, it may not follow that God is a person since God may be conscious but still fail to have the capacity for a robust first-person perspective.

5.3 Personhood, Pantheism, and the *Self-other* Distinction

If we suppose that the capacity for having a robust first-person perspective is essential to being a person, it may be argued that God lacks the capacity for such a first-person perspective on pantheism. This kind of argument is presented by Paul Tillich, who argues that the "basic ontological structure of self and world is transcended in the divine life." He maintains that "God cannot be called a self, because the concept of 'self' implies separation from and contrast to everything which is not self" (Tillich 1951, 244). He asserts that anything that is an object of our ultimate concern cannot be less than personal, so the *symbol* of a "personal God" is important. But, Tillich notes, "since personality ... includes individuality, the question arises in what sense God can be called an individual." He asserts that it is only meaningful to assert that God is the "absolute individual" insofar as God can also be labeled as the "absolute participant" (1951, 244–245).

Whether or not Tillich is best interpreted as a pantheist or a panentheist or as endorsing an entirely different conception of God is unimportant for my purposes here. The general line of reasoning presented can be modified to render an argument against personal pantheism. The argument is quite simple (note that I am taking "God" to pick out God as characterized by pantheism).

1. God lacks a first-person perspective because nothing is genuinely "other" for God.
2. If (1), then God lacks a first-person perspective.
3. If God lacks a first-person perspective, then God is not a person.
4. So, God is not a person.

Notice that God can be conscious, but God's conscious experiences are quite different from ours, involving no *self-other* distinction.

I believe that, in many respects, this kind of argument presents a greater challenge than the previous one. Notice that there is no assumption that God lacks a mind or that the divine mind lacks a capacity for conscious experience. The point is one about the capacity for a certain kind of conscious experience that would be characteristic of having a first-person perspective.

There are two features of Peter Forrest's personal pantheism that could help us here. First, Forrest suggests that the kind of awareness that is characteristic of divine consciousness is proprioceptive. "Assuming God is aware of the universe, ... God knows [the universe] like we know our bodies" (Forrest 2016, 28). Forrest holds that there is pervasive awareness of all things in the universe on this view (2016, 31). Notice that in proprioception there is no *self-other* distinction, but there is a representation of oneself and some parts of oneself. But there is room on this account for a robust divine first-person perspective if God's self-consciousness involves awareness of some states of God's body that are represented first-personally.

While I think this alone would be a promising reply to Tillich, Forrest's account has more resources to aid in responding to the sort of reasoning Tillich's argument represents. On Forrest's personal pantheism, conscious entities (such as humans and other animals) are like so many holes in the divine person. Importantly, it is each center of consciousness (and not the entire object that is, say, a cat or a human) that is like a hole in God (see subsection 4.4 for details). Ergo, Forrest's personal pantheism allows for another dimension to God's first-person perspective. If Forrest is right, then God stands in a *self-other* relation to us *qua* centers of conscious cognition. Assuming the success of Forrest's strategy, the threat posed by the Tillich-inspired argument appears to be a chimera for the personal pantheist.

5.4 Linguistic Communities, Mental Content, and Personhood

The final objection to personal pantheism was developed by Simon Hewitt (2019) and proceeds from some controversial assumptions about the intentionality of mental content. Hewitt suggests that there are three broad approaches to answering the question "what is required for the possession of contentful states?": *mind-first*, *language-first*, and *no-priority* views (2019, 288). Where they differ is on the conditions that must be satisfied to be in a contentful-state. By "mind-first views," Hewitt appears to be referring to internalist accounts of mental content that prioritize having mental states for having contentful-states. "Language-first views' picks out externalist accounts of mental content that prioritize being part of a linguistic community. No-priority views hold that one must have both mental states and have some understanding of a language (Hewitt 2019, 288). Hewitt contends that "God, as conceived of by pantheism, cannot have a grasp of a language and so cannot, on either a language first or a no priority view, be the subject of contentful states (and so, cannot be a person)" (2019, 288). Hewitt claims that an "unfortunate result" for the personal pantheist is that they are then "hostage to the correctness of a mind-first account of content" (2019, 288).

The problem that Hewitt identifies stems from externalist assumptions about mental content on which the meaning of the content of one's mental states depends upon the external world, including one's linguistic community from which one inherits the rules of language use. Assuming that mental content cannot be possessed by anyone who is not a member of a linguistic community, Hewitt asserts that the pantheistic God cannot be a member of a linguistic community. So, if God is not a member of a linguistic community, then God lacks contentful mental states. Therefore, God is not a person (Hewitt 2019, 290–291).

I think there are good reasons to endorse what Hewitt refers to as "mind-first views" that are independent of a commitment to pantheism as the most plausible metaphysics of the divine. Considerations of space will not allow me to visit all of the reasons that might be offered for endorsing internalism about mental content. But there are three responses to Hewitt, each of which I take to be individually sufficient to cast serious doubt on the tenability of his thesis. The first is about what Hewitt assumes about God's relation to linguistic communities. The second and third will be quick and are both directed at some controversial assumptions Hewitt makes about mental content.

Hewitt considers the following response from a would-be interlocutor. In response to the question Hewitt asks about who the other members of God's linguistic community would be, he considers a response to the effect that "God communicates linguistically with God's proper parts" (2019, 290). Such communication would require a linguistic give-and-take. This is missing, according to Hewitt. In the case of ourselves, he notes that "I might argue with myself in my internal monologues, but it is myself I am arguing with" (Hewitt 2019, 290). So also, any engagement by God with a proper part of God "is not second-personal" (2019, 290). Hewitt writes that such a scenario "is one in which a proper part of a person has reasons distinct from those possessed by the person in question and which may be articulated over and against that person" (2019, 290–291). Hewitt maintains that any reasons had by a proper part P of a whole S would be reasons of S's.

> In the normal course of things we can recognise distinctness of reasons amongst dialogue partners through their having disjoint animal lives. That basis for distinction is absent here, and so unless there is another basis for distinction, we should not admit the possibility that the part's reasons are not reasons for the whole. (Hewitt 2019, 291)

Notice that Hewitt's reasoning here rests on two assumptions. First, that any persons *qua* cognitive systems are proper parts of God whose cognitive lives are not uniquely theirs in some sense. Second, if something is a proper part of something else, the whole inherits characteristics from its proper parts in such a way as to eliminate any distinction between the whole and its parts with respect to that characteristic.

First, that you and I *qua* conscious cognitive systems are proper parts of God whose cognitive lives are not uniquely theirs is not uncontroversial. If Forrest is right, then while in God (and even being such that we could be regarded as proper parts of God), we have distinct cognitive lives that can be individuated on the basis of the degree of unity exhibited in those regions where we are. Owing to our status as distinctive cognitive systems, our give-and-take with God is not like an internal dialogue we might have with ourselves. So, God could be part of a linguistic community with other persons.

Suppose we reject Forrest's version of personal pantheism; do we have to agree with Hewitt and abandon personal pantheism? Not obviously. Hewitt assumes that if I am a proper part of God, then if I have a reason for A-ing, God has a reason for A-ing. I worry that Hewitt's argument is based on the fallacy of composition. If God's perspective is that of the whole that is a functionally integrated conscious cognitive system, the cognitive processing of that system would be on a cosmic scale. The reasons of the whole might include reasons of the parts if the whole identifies with those reasons, but it does not follow that the reasons of the proper parts are now reasons of the whole. What Hewitt assumes is that the reasons processed by the cognitive systems that are proper parts of the whole and the outputs of those parts cannot fail to be endorsed by the whole. But it seems perfectly reasonable for a system that is a whole to consider an output or reason considered by one of its proper parts (that is itself a cognitive system) and fail to endorse either the output or the reason that generated it.

This brings me to two further problems with Hewitt's argument. The first is that he appears to assume that all intentional mental content is linguistic in form. If we accept this view, then the only animals with whom we interact who have cognitive lives are language users (specifically, humans). But not all representational content is linguistic. It all involves imagery of some sort. Some of that imagery is linguistic. But it need not be. Language use certainly enriches the content of our mental states. But even language is imagistic – linguistic content involves linguistic imagery.[26] Failure to acknowledge this will result in accepting the claim that nonlanguage users fail to have contentful mental states. Any such assumption seems based on an unjustifiable set of anthropocentric assumptions. If this is right, and God is not a part of a linguistic community (assuming the correctness of Hewitt's assumption for linguistic content), then God could still have intentional mental states.

Finally, at least for the proponent of the powers-based approach, intentionality is fundamental. I will not restate the reasons that I discussed in subsection 4.4 in favor of this claim. I will note that any considerations that favor the powers-based approach discussed in subsection 4.4 will be reasons that count in favor of what Hewitt refers to as "mind-first views." Heil's remarks here about the connection between powers/dispositional properties are instructive. "Intelligent agents are … complex dispositional systems; thinkers are agents with appropriately focused dispositional makeups. Dispositionality underlies the projective character of thought" (Heil 2004, 289). There is more I can say about these matters. For now, I hope it is clear that, even if Hewitt is right about God and linguistic communities, it does not obviously follow that God cannot have contentful mental states.

5.5 Where Does This Leave Us?

I have not attempted to offer reasons for thinking the pantheistic God is a person. My main goal here has been to show that personal pantheism is not incoherent and that it is a live option for us to consider accepting. I have not tried to offer even a *prima facie* case for accepting personal pantheism. But I do hope that I have offered some reasons for readers to consider personal pantheism as a live option. I do not think that the success of pantheism as a viable

---

[26] My thinking here is influenced by Heil 2012 and Martin 2007.

metaphysics of the divine rests on the success of personal pantheism. But, again, it is a position that is attractive, even if it proves ultimately untenable.

6 Conclusion

Pantheism has received far less attention than variants of traditional theism in analytic philosophy of religion. I have focused narrowly on a set of considerations revolving around how we should understand pantheism and its general conceptual and ontological commitments. So, I have not been able to take up issues such as what, if any, of the traditional omniproperties God might have on pantheism or the problem of evil for pantheism, among other issues. Additionally, I have not tried to make a case for accepting pantheism, *per se*. That said, I do hope that readers recognize it as a coherent conception of God that is worthy of investigation and deeper engagement by analytic philosophers of religion. There has been an uptick of interest in pantheism and other alternatives to traditional theism in recent years. This is a promising trend. I hope it will continue unabated going into the future.

References

Adams, F. and Garrison, R. (2013) The mark of the cognitive. *Minds and Machines*, **23**, 339–352.

Alter, T. and Nagasawa, Y. (2015) What is Russellian monism? In T. Alter and Y. Nagasawa (eds.) *Consciousness in the physical world: perspectives on Russellian monism* (422–451). New York: Oxford University Press.

Alter, T. and Pereboom, D. (2019) Russellian monism. In E. Zalta (ed.), *The Stanford encyclopedia of philosophy* (Fall 2019 edition). https://plato.stanford.edu/archives/fall2019/entries/russellian-monism/

Anselm of Canterbury (1066/1998) Monologion. S. Harrison (trans.). In B. Davies (ed.) *Anselm of Canterbury: the major works* (5–81). New York: Oxford University Press.

Aranyosi, I. (2013) *God, mind, and logical space*. New York: Palgrave Macmillan.

Armstrong, D. (1999) A naturalist program: epistemology and ontology. *Proceedings and Addresses of the American Philosophical Association*, **73**, 77–89.

Baker, L. (2013) *Naturalism and the first-person perspective*. New York: Oxford University Press.

Baltzly, D. (2003) Stoic pantheism. *Sophia*, **42**, 3–33.

Bauer, W. (2019) Powers and the pantheistic problem of unity. *Sophia*, **58**, 563–580.

Bishop, J. (1998) Can there be alternative concepts of God? *Noûs*, **32**, 174–188.

Borghini, A. and Williams, N. (2008) A dispositional theory of possibility. *Dialectica*, **62**, 21–41.

Buckareff, A. (2012) Omniscience, the incarnation, and knowledge de se. *European Journal for Philosophy of Religion*, **4**, 59–71.

Buckareff, A. (2016) Pantheism and saving God. *Sophia*, **55**, 347–355.

Buckareff, A. (2018) Theistic consubstantialism and omniscience. *Religious Studies*, **54**, 233–245.

Buckareff, A. (2019) Unity, ontology, and the divine mind. *International Journal for Philosophy of Religion*, **85**, 319–333.

Byerly, T. R. (2019) The awe-some argument for pantheism. *European Journal for Philosophy of Religion*, **11**, 1–21.

Calvin, J. (1559/1960) *Institutes of the Christian religion*, 2 vols. J. T. McNeill (ed.) F. L. Battles (trans.). Philadelphia: The Westminster Press.

Cameron, R. (2008) Truthmakers and ontological commitment: or how to deal with complex objects and mathematical ontology without getting into trouble. *Philosophical Studies*, **140**, 1–18.

Chalmers, D. (1995) Facing up to the problem of consciousness. *Journal of Consciousness Studies*, **2**, 200–219.

Chalmers, D. (2017a) Panpsychism and panprotopsychism. In G. Brüntrup and L. Jaskolla (eds.) *Panpsychism: contemporary perspectives* (19–47). New York: Oxford University Press.

Chalmers, D. (2017b) The combination problem for panpsychism. In G. Brüntrup and L. Jaskolla (eds.) *Panpsychism: contemporary perspectives* (179–214). New York: Oxford University Press.

Chisholm, R. (1981) Defining intrinsic value. *Analysis*, **41**, 99–100.

Coleman, S. (2019) Personhood, consciousness, and god: how to be a proper pantheist. *International Journal for Philosophy of Religion*, **85**, 77–98.

Curley, E. (1969) *Spinoza's metaphysics: an essay in interpretation*. Cambridge: Harvard University Press.

Davies, B. (2016) Aquinas on what God is not. *Philosophy*, **78**, 55–71.

Effingham, N. (2021) The CaML model of pantheism. *Religious Studies*, **57**, 575–596.

Esfeld, M. (2012) Causal realism. In D. Dieks, W. Gonzalez, S. Hartmann, M. Stöltzner, and M. Weber (eds.) *Probabilities, laws and structures* (157–168). Dordrecht: Springer.

Forrest, P. (2007) *Developmental theism: from pure will to unbounded love*. New York: Oxford University Press.

Forrest, P. (2016) The personal pantheist conception of God. In A. Buckareff and Y. Nagasawa (eds.) *Alternative concepts of God: essays on the metaphysics of the divine* (21–41). New York: Oxford University Press.

Fredkin, E. (2003) An introduction to digital philosophy. *International Journal of Theoretical Physics*, **42**, 189–247.

Friedlander, M. (1888) *Spinoza: his life and philosophy*. London: Jewish Chronicle Office.

Goff, P. (2017a) *Consciousness and fundamental reality*. New York: Oxford University Press.

Goff, P. (2017b) The phenomenal bonding solution to the combination problem. In G. Brüntrup and L. Jaskolla (eds.) *Panpsychism: contemporary perspectives* (283–302). New York: Oxford University Press.

Goff, P. (2019) Did the universe design itself? *International Journal for Philosophy of Religion*, **85**, 99–122.

Goff, P., Seager, W. and Allen-Hermanson, S. (2020) Panpsychism. In E. Zalta (ed.) *Stanford encyclopedia of philosophy* (Summer 2020 edition). https://plato.stanford.edu/archives/sum2020/entries/panpsychism/

Hartshorne, C. (1948) *The divine relativity: a social conception of God*. New Haven: Yale University Press.

Heil, J. (1998) Supervenience deconstructed. *European Journal of Philosophy*, **6**, 146–155.

Heil, J. (2003) *From an ontological point of view*. New York: Oxford University Press.

Heil, J. (2004) Natural intentionality. In R. Schantz (ed.) *The externalist challenge* (287–296). New York: De Gruyter.

Heil, J. (2012) *The universe as we find it*. New York: Oxford University Press.

Heil, J. (2020) Ontology of powers. In A. Meincke (ed.) *Dispositionalism: perspectives from metaphysics and the philosophy of science* (13–26). Cham: Springer.

Hewitt, S. (2019) God is not a person (an argument *via* pantheism). *International Journal for Philosophy of Religion*, **85**, 281–296.

Hick, J. (1989) *An interpretation of religion: human responses to the transcendent*. New Haven: Yale University Press.

Horgan, T. and Potrc, M. (2008) *Austere realism: contextual semantics meets minimal ontology*. Cambridge, MA: The MIT Press.

Hudson, H. (2009) Omnipresence. In M. Rea (ed.) *The Oxford handbook of philosophical Theology* (199–216). New York: Oxford University Press.

Jacobs, J. (2011) Powerful qualities, not pure powers. *The Monist*, **94**, 81–102.

James, W. (1890/1950) *The principles of psychology*, vol. I. New York: Dover.

Jantzen, G. (1978) On worshipping an embodied God. *Canadian Journal of Philosophy*, **8**, 511–519.

Jantzen, G. (1984) *God's world, God's body*. Philadelphia: The Westminster Press.

Jaskolla, L. and Buck, A. (2012) Does panexperiential holism solve the combination problem? *Journal of Consciousness Studies*, **19**, 190–199.

Johnston, M. (2007) Objective mind and the objectivity of our minds. *Philosophy and Phenomenological Research*, **75**, 233–268.

Johnston, M. (2009) *Saving God: religion after idolatry*. Princeton: Princeton University Press.

Laird, J. (1941) *Mind and deity*. New York: Routledge.

Lancaster-Thomas, A. (2020) The coherence of naturalistic personal pantheism. *European Journal for Philosophy of Religion*, **12**, 75–89.

Leftow, B. (2016) Naturalistic pantheism. In A. Buckareff and Y. Nagasawa (eds.) *Alternative concepts of God: essays on the metaphysics of the divine* (64–90). New York: Oxford University Press.

Leidenhag, J. (2019) Unity between God and mind? A study on the relationship between panpsychism and pantheism. *Sophia*, **58**, 543–561.

Leslie, J. (2001) *Infinite minds: a philosophical cosmology*. New York: Oxford University Press.

Leslie, J. (2015) God and many universes. In K. Kraay (ed.) *God and the multiverse: scientific, and theological perspectives* (192–207). New York: Routledge.

Levine, M. (1994) *Pantheism: a non-theistic concept of deity*. New York: Routledge.

Lloyd, S. (2006) *Programming the universe: A quantum computer scientist takes on the cosmos*. New York: Knopf.

Lloyd, S. (2010) Taking a byte out of the universe. *New Scientist*, **205**, 46.

Lockwood, M. (1989) *Mind, brain, and the quantum: the compound "I"*. Oxford: Blackwell.

MacIntyre, A. (1967/2006) Pantheism. In D. Borchert (ed.) *Encyclopedia of philosophy*, 2nd ed., vol. 7 (94–98). New York: Macmillan.

Maimonides, M. (1190/1904) *The guide for the perplexed*, 2nd ed. M. Friedländer (trans.). London: Routledge and Kegan Paul, Ltd.

Mander, W. (2007) Theism, pantheism, and petitionary prayer. *Religious Studies*, **43**, 317–331.

Mander, W. (2020) Pantheism. In E. Zalta (ed.) *The Stanford encyclopedia of philosophy*. https://plato.stanford.edu/archives/spr2020/entries/pantheism/

Marmodoro, A. (2017) Power mereology: structural powers *versus* substantial powers. In M.P. Paoletti and F. Orilia (eds.) *Philosophical and scientific perspectives on downward causation* (110–128). New York: Routledge.

Martin, C. B. (2007) *The mind in nature*. New York: Oxford University Press.

Meinong, A. (1904/1960) The theory of objects. In R. M. Chisholm (ed.) *Realism and the background of phenomenology* (76–117). Atascadero, CA: Ridgeview.

Melamed, Y. (2013) *Spinoza's metaphysics: substance and thought*. New York: Oxford University Press.

Melamed, Y. (2018) Cohen, Spinoza and the nature of pantheism. *Jewish Studies Quarterly*, **25**, 1–10.

Molnar, G. (2003) *Powers: a study in metaphysics*. New York: Oxford University Press.

Moore, G. E. (1903) *Principia Ethica*. New York: Cambridge University Press.

Mørch, H. (2020) Does dispositionalism entail panpsychism? *Topoi*, **39**, 1073–1088.

Mumford, S. (1998) *Dispositions*. New York: Oxford University Press.

Nagasawa, Y. (2015) Multiverse pantheism. In K. Kraay (ed.) *God and the multiverse: scientific, philosophical, and theological perspectives* (177–191). New York: Routledge.

Nagasawa, Y. (2020) Panpsychism versus pantheism, polytheism, and cosmopsychism. In W. Seager (ed.) *The Routledge handbook of panpsychism* (259–268). New York: Routledge.

Nagasawa, Y. and Wager, K. (2017) Panpsychism and priority cosmopsychism. In G. Brüntrup and L. Jaskolla (eds.) *Panpsychism: contemporary perspectives* (113–129). New York: Oxford University Press.

Nozick, R. (1981) *Philosophical explanations*. Cambridge, MA: Harvard University Press.

Oakes, R. (2006) Divine omnipresence and maximal immanence: supernaturalism versus pantheism. *American Philosophical Quarterly*, **43**, 171–179.

Oakes, R. (2012) Strong interiority and (traditional) theism: what's the problem? *Ratio*, **25**, 68–78.

Oppy, G. (1997) Pantheism, quantification, and mereology. *The Monist*, **80**, 320–36.

Page, B. (2019) Wherein lies the debate? Concerning whether God is a person. *International Journal for Philosophy of Religion*, **85**, 297–317.

Pexton, M. (2015) Emergence and fundamentality in a pancomputational universe. *Minds and Machines*, **25**, 301–320.

Pfeifer, K. (2016) Pantheism as panpsychism. In A. Buckareff and Y. Nagasawa (eds.) *Alternative concepts of God: essays on the metaphysics of the divine* (41–49). New York: Oxford University Press.

Piccinini, G. (2015) *Physical computation: a mechanistic account*. New York: Oxford University Press.

Pruss, A. (2013) Omnipresence, multilocation, the real presence, and time travel. *Journal of Analytic Theology*, **1**, 60–73.

Schaffer, J. (2009) Spacetime the one substance. *Philosophical Studies*, **145**, 131–148.

Schaffer, J. (2010) Monism: the priority of the whole. *The Philosophical Review*, **119**, 31–76.

Schellenberg, J. L. (2005) *Prolegomena to a philosophy of religion*. Ithaca: Cornell University Press.

Schellenberg, J. L. (2009) *The will to imagine: a justification of skeptical religion*. Ithaca: Cornell University Press.

Seager, W. (1995) Consciousness, information, and panpsychism. *Journal of Consciousness Studies*, **2**, 272–288.

Searle, J. (1980) Minds, brains, and programs. *Behavioral and Brain Sciences*, **3**, 417–57.

Spinoza, B. (1662/1985) Letter 6: B. D. S. to the most noble and learned Henry Oldenburg. In E. Curley (ed. and trans.) *The collected works of Spinoza*, vol 1. (173–188). Princeton, NJ: Princeton University Press.

Spinoza, B. (1677/1985) Ethics. In E. Curley (ed. and trans.) *The collected works of Spinoza*, vol 1. (401–617). Princeton, NJ: Princeton University Press.

Sprigge, T. L. S. (2006) *The God of metaphysics*. New York: Oxford University Press.

Steinhart, E. (2004) Pantheism and current ontology. *Religious Studies*, **40**, 63–80.

Suttle, G. (2008) Raphson, Joseph (1648–1715). In B. Taylor (ed.) *Encyclopedia of religion and nature* (1341–1342). London: Bloomsbury.

Swinburne, R. (1993) *The coherence of theism*, revised edition. New York: Oxford University Press.

Thatcher, A. (1985) The personal God and a God who is not a person. *Religious Studies*, **21**, 61–73.

Tillich, P. (1951) *Systematic theology*, vol. 1. Chicago: University of Chicago Press.

Tononi, G. and Koch, C. (2015) Consciousness: here, there, and everywhere? *Philosophical Transactions of the Royal Society B*, **370**, 1–18.

Vazza, F. and Feletti, A. (2020) The quantitative comparison between the neuronal network and the cosmic web. *Frontiers in Physics*, **8**, 1–8. doi: 10.3389/fphy.2020.525731

Wang, J. (2016) The nature of properties: causal essentialism and quidditism. *Philosophy Compass*, **11**, 168–176.

Wettstein, H. (1997) Awe and the religious life: A naturalistic perspective. *Midwest Studies in Philosophy*, **21**, 257–280.

Whitehead, A. (1929) *Process and reality: an essay in cosmology*. New York: Macmillan.

Acknowledgments

I wish to thank Yujin Nagasawa for both inviting me to write this Element and for the many conversations we have had for over a decade about alternative conceptions of God that have helped shape my thinking about pantheism. Thanks are also due to two anonymous reviewers for Cambridge University Press who offered incisive feedback on an earlier draft of this Element. In working on this project, I have benefitted from conversations with and feedback from too many people to remember. But I am especially grateful to the following people for conversations and/or feedback on this Element and on related work: John Bishop, Andrew Chignell, Peter Forrest, Philip Goff, Asha Lancaster-Thomas, Ken Perszyk, and Jack Symes. I wish to thank my spouse, Lara Kasper-Buckareff, and my son, Soren Buckareff, for their unconditional love, support, and patience with me as I worked on this project. Work on this project was supported, in part, by a grant from the John Templeton Foundation (#59140: "The Pantheism and Panentheism Project") and by the provision of course releases by Marist College. Finally, I wish to dedicate this Element to the memory of my late mentor, teacher, and friend, Hugh J. McCann.

Cambridge Elements $\equiv$

Philosophy of Religion

Yujin Nagasawa

University of Birmingham

Yujin Nagasawa is Professor of Philosophy and Co-director of the John Hick Centre for Philosophy of Religion at the University of Birmingham. He is currently President of the British Society for the Philosophy of Religion. He is a member of the Editorial Board of *Religious Studies*, the *International Journal for Philosophy of Religion*, and *Philosophy Compass*.

About the Series

This Cambridge Elements series provides concise and structured introductions to all the central topics in the philosophy of religion. It offers balanced, comprehensive coverage of multiple perspectives in the philosophy of religion. Contributors to the series are cutting-edge researchers who approach central issues in the philosophy of religion. Each provides a reliable resource for academic readers and develops new ideas and arguments from a unique viewpoint.

Cambridge Elements $\equiv$

Philosophy of Religion

A full series listing is available at: www.cambridge.org/EPREL

Printed in the United States
by Baker & Taylor Publisher Services